Thistle
Guide 2
GOBLINSHEAD

Castles
of Scotland

Martin Coventry

GOBLINSHEAD

Musselburgh

W9-BHP-906

Castles of Scotland
First published 2005
© Martin Coventry 2005
Developed, updated and expanded from
Wee Guide to the Castles and Mansions of Scotland
© Martin Coventry 1998

Published by GOBLINSHEAD
130B Inveresk Road, Musselburgh EH21 7AY
Tel: 0131 665 2894; fax: 0131 653 6566
Email: goblinshead@sol.co.uk

British Library Cataloguing in Publication Data
A catalogue record for this book is available from
the British Library.

ISBN 1 899874 24 0

Printed by Bell & Bain, Glasgow, Scotland

Already published in the Thistle Guide series:
Churches and Abbeys of Scotland (1899874291; £5.95)

If you would like a colour catalogue of our
publications please contact:
Goblinshead, 130B Inveresk Road,
Musselburgh EH21 7AY, Scotland, UK.

Disclaimer:
The information contained in this Castles of Scotland
(the "Material") is believed to be accurate at the time of printing, but no
representation or warranty is given (express or implied) as to its accuracy,
completeness or correctness. The author and publisher do not accept any
liability whatsoever for any direct, indirect or consequential loss or
damage arising in any way from any use of or reliance on this Material
for any purpose.

While every care has been taken to compile and check all the information
in this book, in a work of this complexity it is possible that mistakes and
omissions may have occurred. If you know of any corrections, alterations or
improvements, please contact the publishers at the address above.

Contents

How to use this book

There is a brief introduction to castle and mansions in Scotland (pages 1-7), which is followed by a map locating all the sites (pages 8-9).

The main part (pages 10-110) of the book has 200 castles, tower houses, stately homes, mansions and historic houses which are open to the public. Each entry begins with the name of the site and whether it is in the care of Historic Scotland (HS) or The National Trust for Scotland (NTS). This is followed by its reference number on the map along with its grid reference in square brackets (of the form [*Map: 2; H6*]). This is followed by the location, national grid reference (NGR) and the OS Landranger map number (LR). There is then a description of the site, along with facilities including an indication of admission price (£<£3.50, ££=£3.50-5.00, £££>£5.00), opening times and contact details (telephone and websites).

A small section follows this, listing some places which offer accommodation (pages 111-116): some sites in the main part also do this.

There is then a glossary of terms (pages 117-118), an index by family or clan (page 119) and a main index (pages 120-122). Bold entries refer to places featured in the main text (not in the places to stay), a bold page number refers to the first page of the entry, and an underlined page number refers to an illustration (**Tolquhon Castle 107**: the main entry for Tolquhon is on page 107 and there is also an illustration on that page).

Selected further reading

Black, George F. *The Surnames of Scotland*, New York, 1946

Connachan-Holme, J R A *Country Houses of Scotland*, Frome, 1995

Coventry, Martin *Castles of Scotland,* third edn, Musselburgh, 2001

Coventry, Martin *Haunted Castles and Houses of Scotland*, Musselburgh, 2004

Dewar, Peter Beauclerk *Burke's Landed Gentry of Great Britain: The Kingdom in Scotland,* 19th edn, Wilmington, 2001

Groome, Francis *Ordnance Gazetteer of Scotland* (5 vols), Glasgow, 1890

Lindsay, Maurice *The Castles of Scotland*, London, 1986

MacGibbon, D & Ross, T *The Castellated and Domestic Architecture of Scotland*, 1887-1892

Mason, Gordon *The Castles of Glasgow and the Clyde*, Musselburgh 2000

McKean, Charles (ed.) *Illustrated Architectural Guides*, Edinburgh, from 1985 *(Series of books covering most of Scotland)*

Salter, Mike *The Castles of South West Scotland*, Worcester, 1993

Salter, Mike *The Castles of the Heartland of Scotland*, Worcester, 1994

Salter, Mike *The Castles of Lothian and the Borders*, Worcester, 1994

Salter, Mike *The Castles of Western and Northwest Scotland*, Worcester, 1995

Salter, Mike *The Castles of Grampian and Angus*, Worcester, 1993

Tabraham, Mike *Scotland's Castles*, London, 1997

Tranter, Nigel *The Fortified House in Scotland*, Edinburgh, 1986

Way of Plean, George & Squire, Romilly *Scottish Clan & Family Encyclopedia*, Glasgow, 1994

Guidebooks are available for many of the castles and mansions which are open to the public.

Preface

This second volume in the Thistle Guide series is a compact guide to the all the best castles, tower houses, royal palaces, mansions and stately homes which are open to the public and can be visited. This has been limited to some 200 sites, plus another fifty which offer accommodation (as, of course, do some of the places in the main text).

It is always difficult to limit numbers, and I have tried to include as wide a selection of places as possible: massive fortresses and grand mansions right through to shattered and fragmentary ruins, albeit in beautiful locations. I am also aware that many of the most popular sites have substantial (and it appears rapidly increasing) entry charges, so also included are many castles which are free – although these tend to have few or no facilities.

As mentioned elsewhere, if it is intended to visit many castles and mansions it may be worth joining, even if just in purely monetary terms, The National Trust for Scotland (NTS) and Historic Scotland (HS): contact details are included on page 10. These two institutions have most of the best castles in their care: NTS castles or mansions are usually complete and are furnished, and they also manage many gardens and estates; while Historic Scotland has many fabulous ruins, along with the great castles of Stirling and Edinburgh, abbeys, churches, prehistoric sites and even a distillery.

Although *Castles of Scotland* is a small book (at least in format), it does contain a large amount of information and, while I have tried to check everything (either by phone or on websites), mistakes or omissions will have occurred. Please contact me if you think it could be improved or I have been remiss in not including any sites or information has changed. We have been accused of packing too much into our books and, making no apology for this, room can usually be found for new or improved information.

This new book owes much to its bigger brother *The Castles of Scotland*, third edition, which is currently sold out. I am aware that this is very expensive and not everyone has the interest or pocket for such a large and all encompassing work. The bigger brother is now coming into its fourth edition, and should be available towards the end of 2005 or in 2006.

Thistle Guides are intended to be both portable and detailed, delivering a substantial amount of information on a topic in a handy, compact format. Our first offering was *Churches and Abbeys of Scotland*, which was published in 2003, has been well received and reviewed. It has taken rather longer to get out *Castles of Scotland* than I would have liked. We are, however, hoping to bring out further titles in 2006/7, and topics to be published include brochs, forts and duns; standing stones, cairns and tombs; and lighthouses.

MC, Musselburgh, May 2005

The front cover photograph is of the great castle of Kildrummy, while those on the back cover are of Holyrood Palace in Edinburgh, Brodick Castle on Arran and Eilean Donan Castle on the road to Skye.

Introduction

One of the main functions of the castle was obviously defensive: to protect the lord and his family from their enemies, but in as comfortable and impressive surroundings as possible. The castle was the centre of

Craigmillar Castle

administration, from where tenure, economy and trade were controlled, law dispensed, and wrongdoers punished. Originally a large stronghold could defend against an invading army, but by the 16th century the increased use of effective artillery pieces made castles redundant as major strong-points. By then the defensive capabilities of most strongholds were relegated to the protection of the owners from raids or attacks by bands of brigands or neighbours. As times became more peaceful, many castles were abandoned for comfortable and spacious mansions, or were extended by wings and ranges of buildings.

MOTTE AND BAILEY CASTLES (12TH CENTURY)

During the 12th century, motte and bailey castles were introduced along with feudalism into Scotland, mostly into Lowland areas. Motte and bailey castles are mostly concentrated in Clydesdale, Galloway and Grampian. Galloway was unruly at the time, and these castles were built to subdue the area: although their introduction does not seem to have worked very well. There appear to have been few motte and bailey castle in places such as central Scotland, the Lothians and the Highlands.

These castles consisted of an earthen mound, known as a motte, and a courtyard, or bailey, enclosed by a wooden palisade and defended by a ditch. The plan of the motte was usually round, but some were also oval or rectangular. At the base of the motte was a dry or wet ditch or moat.

A wooden tower was built on the motte, where the lord and his followers could shelter if attacked. The bailey contained many buildings, such as the hall, chapel, kitchen, bakehouse and stables. Wooden castles were not used for long, as they could be set alight, but had the advantage of being easy and quick to build.

Often all that remains today is evidence of the earthworks, some good examples of these being Motte of Urr, Druchtag, Coulter, and the Peel Ring of Lumphanan. Duffus and Rothesay are two of the few examples where a stone keep was added. Other mottes and their surrounding earthworks were reused by later castle builders.

STONE CASTLES (12TH CENTURY-)

Stone castles were built from the 12th century in Scotland, although stone-built duns and brochs – stone enclosures or round towers – had been used since before the birth of Christ.

The simplest form was a wall enclosing a two-storey hall block of wood or stone. The entrance to the hall block was on the first floor, and was reached by a ladder, which could be removed easily during attack. The wall was usually surrounded by a ditch and rampart.

Good examples of early castles include Cubbie Roo's Castle on Orkney, Castle Sween and Old Castle of Wick.

By the 13th century, walls were heightened and strengthened, enclosing a courtyard which contained both the hall and lord's chamber, as well as kitchens, bakeries, brewhouses, stables and storerooms. Corner towers were added to defend the castle. The walls were pierced by slits through which crossbows could be fired. Castles dating at least in part from this time include Balvenie, Crookston, Duart, Dundonald, Dunstaffnage, Inverlochy, Loch Doon, Skipness and Urquhart.

Strong gatehouses were added with portcullises, drawbridges, iron-studded doors, and murder-holes. The curtain walls were given battlements for archers to shelter behind. By the 14th century, large stone castles such as Bothwell, Caerlaverock and Kildrummy had been built.

These consisted of a keep – a large strong tower with a hall and chambers for the lord – and thick curtain walls with round or square corner towers.

There are relatively few very large castles left in Scotland, partly due to the expense of constructing and maintaining such buildings, and partly because many were destroyed by the Scots during the Wars of Independence. Strong royal castles were maintained, including those at Edinburgh, Stirling, Dumbarton, Roxburgh and Dunbar – although little

Bothwell Castle

remains of the last two. A few of the most powerful families could also afford massive fortresses, such as the Douglas strongholds of Tantallon and Threave, and the Keith stronghold of Dunnottar.

Keeps (14th/15th century)

These castles consisted of a square or rectangular tower and an adjoining courtyard. The walls of the keep were thick, and normally rose through at least three storeys to a flush crenellated parapet. The basement and first floor were vaulted to increase the strength of the building. The size of the keep depended on the wealth of the builder.

The basement contained a cellar, often with no connection to the floor above. The hall was on the first floor, with a private chamber for the lord on the floor above, and a garret storey above this. The thick walls contained many mural chambers, either small bedrooms or garderobes. The entrance was at first-floor level, and was reached by an external stair. Stairs led up, within the walls, to each floor. The keep was roofed with stone slates, or slabs, to protect it against attack by fire.

The courtyard enclosed buildings such as a kitchen, stables, chapel, brewhouse, and was surrounded by a wall often with a ditch and drawbridge.

Large castles which date substantially from this period are numerous – although most have been altered or extended in later centuries – and include Aberdour, Alloa, Balgonie, Cardoness, Castle Campbell, Castle

Aberdour Castle

Stalker, Cawdor, Craigmillar, Crichton, Delgatie, Doune, Drummond, Dunrobin, Dunvegan, Eilean Donan, Glamis, Hermitage, Huntingtower, Huntly, Kilchurn, Kilravock, Lennoxlove, Lochleven, Neidpath, Newark, Ravenscraig, Spynie and Tolquhon. Simpler castles of the period include Orchardton and Smailholm.

PALACES (15TH-17TH CENTURY)

The Stewart monarchs built or remodelled the royal palaces in the Renaissance style at Stirling, Holyrood, Linlithgow, Falkland and Dunfermline, creating comfortable residences preferable to royal castles.

TOWER HOUSES (16TH-17TH CENTURY)

In 1535 an Act of Parliament declared that every landed man that had land valued at £100 (Scots) was to build a tower or castle to defend his lands.

Although there is no clear divide, tower houses evolved from keeps, with more consideration being taken of comfort. The walls became less thick, and the entrance was moved to the basement. Parapets were corbelled-out so that they would overhang the wall and missiles could be dropped on attackers below. The corners had open rounds, and the stair was crowned by a caphouse and watch-chamber. Gunloops and shot-holes replaced arrowslits. The walls were harled and often whitewashed. Castles from this period include Broughty, Corgarff, Craignethan, Gilnockie and Lauriston.

L-PLAN TOWER HOUSES (MID 16TH/17TH CENTURY)

The L-plan tower house had a stair-wing added to the main block. The stair was usually turnpike, and climbed only to the hall on the first floor. The upper floors were reached by a turnpike stair in a small stair-turret corbelled out, above first-floor level, in the re-entrant angle. This stair was crowned by a caphouse and watch-chamber. In some cases, the wing contained a stair which climbed to all floors, and sometimes a separate stair-tower stood within the re-entrant angle, and the wing contained chambers.

The defensive features became less obvious. Larger windows were still protected by iron yetts or grills, and gunloops became ornamental. Open rounds were replaced by bartizans, with conical roofs, and parapets were covered. Decorative features, as well as heraldic panels, inscribed lintels, tempera painting and modelled plaster work were introduced. These design features showed French and Italian influences. The tower usually had a small courtyard with ranges of buildings, including a brewhouse, stabling and more accommodation. Often there was a terraced or walled garden and orchards.

The basement was vaulted and contained a kitchen, with a large fireplace; a wine-cellar, with a small stair to the hall above; and other cellars. The hall was on the first floor of the main block with private chambers, on the floors above, and within the garret or attic storey.

Examples of L-plan towers include Balvaird, Barcaldine, Braemar, Crathes, Drumcoltran, Drumlanrig's Tower, Edzell, Greenknowe, Kellie, Scalloway and Scotstarvit.

Z-PLAN TOWER HOUSES (LATE 16TH/17TH CENTURY)

Z-plan tower houses consisted of a main block, with two towers at diagonally opposite corners. One of the towers usually housed a stair,

Glenbuchat Castle

while the other provided more accommodation. Often further wings or ranges were added to the tower making it E-plan. Castles dating substantially from this period include Ballindalloch, Brodie, Castle Fraser, Castle Menzies, Claypotts, Elcho, Glenbuchat, Leith Hall, MacLellan's, and Noltland.

Forts (16th/17th/18th century)

With the advent of more sophisticated artillery, the castle became increasingly redundant as a major defensive structure. As early as the 1540s, forts were being built to withstand attack by cannon. The English constructed forts, during the invasion of Scotland in 1547-50, including those at Roxburgh, Eyemouth and Haddington, which consisted of ramparts and bastions of earth rather than high walls. In the 1650s Cromwell built forts or Citadels, such as those at Ayr, Leith, Perth, Inverlochy, Inverness and Aberdeen. The Hanoverian Government built forts, barracks and roads because of the Jacobite Risings of 1715 and 1745, including those at Fort George, Fort William, Fort Augustus and Ruthven Barracks. Other castles such as Corgarff and Braemar were remodelled with star-shaped outworks.

Mansion Houses

Even before the Jacobite Risings, most new houses had ceased to be fortified, including mansions such as Drumlanrig, Kinross House and Hopetoun House. By the mid 18th century, most new houses, or extensions to existing buildings, were designed in a classical or symmetrical style by architects such as William Adam, and his sons Robert and John. These featured pillars and pilasters, pediments and statues, fine plasterwork and interiors. Many castles were abandoned at this time, because they were cramped, uncomfortable and unfashionable. Gardens became more ornate and elaborate, and houses were surrounded by acres of parkland. Fine buildings of this period include Mellerstain, Floors, Culzean and Duff House.

Largely as a result of Sir Walter Scott reviving interest in a romanticised Scottish past, baronial mansions came into fashion during the 19th century, incorporating or recreating mock castellated features, such as towers and turrets, corbelling and machiolations. Castles were reused, restored, reoccupied, remodelled or recreated by architects such as William Burn, James Gillespie Graham and David Bryce in the 19th century, and Sir Robert Lorimer in the 20th century. Buildings dating from the 19th and 20th centuries include Ayton, Balmoral (holiday home of the Royal family), Blairquhan, Fasque, Mount Stuart House, Scone Palace and Torosay; while buildings which were remodelled and/or extended include Blair, Bowhill, Brodick, Drum, Dunrobin, Dunvegan, and Lauriston.

Abbotsford

Map of Sites (Locations may be approximate)

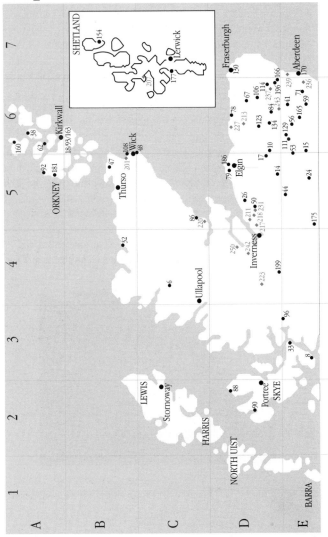

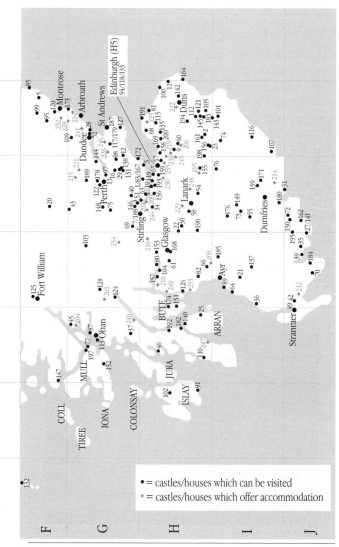

Edinburgh (H5)
94/118/133

● = castles/houses which can be visited
♦ = castles/houses which offer accommodation

Key

Although believed to be correct, information supplied is for basic guidance only, and should be checked with the sites before setting out on any journey. Many castles and tower houses are in inaccessible locations or are dangerously ruined. Inclusion of any site in this book is not a recommendation that it should or can be visited.

Many fine castles are in the care of Historic Scotland and The National Trust for Scotland and, if it is intended to visit many of these, consider joining Historic Scotland and the NTS as, along with other benefits, entry to properties is free for members.

Historic Scotland (HS)
Longmore House, Salisbury Place, Edinburgh EH9 1SH
Tel: 0131 668 8800 Web: www.historic-scotland.gov.uk
The National Trust for Scotland (NTS)
Wemyss House, 28 Charlotte Square, Edinburgh EH2 4ET
Tel: 0131 243 9300 Web: www.nts.org.uk

Kinnaird Head Castle

Abbot House, Dunfermline

[Map: 1; H5] Off A994, just north of Dunfermline Abbey, Maygate, Dunfermline, Fife.
(NGR: NT 089875 LR: 65)

Abbot House is a fine pink-washed building, with two projecting stair-towers, in a pleasant location near Dunfermline Abbey church and the ruins of the palace and domestic buildings. The house dates from the 16th century or earlier, and was used after the Reformation for the commendator of the abbey. Owners have included Anne of Denmark, the wife of James VI; and Lady Anne Halkett, Jacobite, herbalist and mid-wife. Now a heritage centre, Abbot House has displays about the house and about Dunfermline town and abbey, as well as the story of Scotland from Pictish to modern times, including information about St Margaret.

Guided tours. Explanatory displays. Gift shop. Restaurant with outside seating in garden. Garden. WC. Disabled access to ground floor and WC. Disabled parking only; public car parks within 600 yards. Group concessions. £ (Upstairs exhib only).

Open all year, daily 10.00-17.00, last entry 45 miles before closing, closed 25/12 and 1/1.
Tel: 01383 733266   Web: www.abbothouse.co.uk

Abbotsford

[Map: 2; H6] On B6360, 2 miles W of Melrose, Borders. (NGR: NT 508343 LR: 73)

Sir Walter Scott, the famous Scottish writer and historian, bought Cartley Hole farmhouse, by the Tweed, in 1812, which he renamed Abbotsford. He had the old house demolished in 1822, and it was replaced by the main block of Abbotsford as it is today – altered and extended to form a large castellated mansion with turrets, battlements and corbiestepped gables. Scott collected many historic artefacts, and there is an impressive collection of armour and weapons at the house, including Rob Roy MacGregor's gun, a crucifix of Mary Queen of Scots, Claverhouse's pistol and the Marquis of Montrose's sword. There is access to study, library, drawing room, entrance hall and armouries, as well as the dining room, where Scott died in 1832. His library of more than 9000 rare volumes is preserved at the house. There are also extensive gardens and grounds, and private chapel which was added after Scott's death.

The ghost of Sir Walter Scott is said to haunt the dining room, where he died in 1832.

Guided tours. Gift shop. Tearoom. Extensive gardens and grounds. WCs. Disabled access by private entrance. Car and coach parking. Group concessions. ££.

Open daily: 3rd Monday in Mar-Oct, Mon-Sat 9.30-17.00, Sun 14.00-17.00; Jun-Sep, daily including Sun 9.30-17.00; other dates by appt.
Tel: 01896 752043   Web: www.scottsabbotsford.co.uk

Aberdour Castle (HS)

[Map: 3; H5] On A921, 6.5 miles SW of Kirkcaldy, Aberdour, Fife. (NGR: NT 193854 LR: 66)

Standing in the picturesque village, the large castle consists of a ruinous 14th-century keep and ranges of buildings, dating from later centuries, one of which is still roofed and contains a gallery on the first floor. There is also an original painted ceiling. A terraced garden has been restored, and there is also a fine walled garden and round doocot.

Aberdour was a property of the Mortimer family. The stretch of water between the island of Inch Colm and Aberdour is known as 'Mortimer's Deep'. One of the family was a wicked fellow, but wished to be buried at the abbey on Inch Colm. His remains were on their way to the island, but were cast overboard there. The castle had passed to the Douglases by 1342. James Douglas, 4th Earl of Morton, was made Regent for the young James V in 1572. Nine years later, however, the Earl's plotting finally caught up with him, and James VI had him executed. Much of the castle was abandoned in 1725 when the family moved to nearby Aberdour House, although part was used as a barracks, then school room, masonic hall and dwelling until 1924.

The nearby chapel of St Fillan may date from as early as the 12th century.

Explanatory displays. Gift shop. Tearoom. WC. Disabled access and WC. Garden. Parking. £.

Open all year: Apr-Sep, daily 9.30-18.30; Oct-Mar, open Sat-Wed 9.30-16.30, closed Thu-Fri; closed 25/26 Dec and 1/2 Jan.

Tel: 01383 860519

Alloa Tower (NTS)

[Map: 4; G5] Off A907, 7 miles E of Stirling, Alloa, Clackmannan. (NGR: NS 889925 LR: 58)

Standing in a public park, Alloa Tower is a tall imposing keep or tower with very thick walls, and has a rare medieval timber roof. The keep is crowned by a parapet with open rounds, but the building has been much altered by the insertion of large regularly spaced windows and a substantial turnpike stair. A later mansion was finally demolished in 1959.

Alloa was given to Sir Robert Erskine, Great Chamberlain of Scotland, in 1360, and has remained with his descendants until the present day. Mary, Queen of Scots, was reconciled with Darnley here in 1565; and made the family Earls of Mar. John, 6th Earl and known as 'Bobbing John' as he supported first one side and then the other, led the Jacobites rather ineffectually in the 1715 Rising. Although still owned by the Erskines, the tower is now in the care of The National Trust for Scotland.

Explanatory displays. Collection of portraits of the Erskine family. WC. Disabled WC & access to ground floor only. Parking nearby. Group concessions. £.

Open Easter- Oct, daily 13.00-17.00; morning visits available for pre-booked groups.

Tel: 01259 211701

Arbuthnott House

[Map: 5; F6] Off B967, 5.5 miles NE of Laurencekirk, Arbuthnott, Kincardine and Deeside.
(NGR: NO 795750 LR: 45)

On a strong site between two rivers, Arbuthnott House is a large symmetrical mansion with classical detail, but incorporates an old castle. It was extended and remodelled down the years, and some fine ceilings were added about 1685. In the 1750s the gateway side of the courtyard was replaced, and the house remodelled to create a symmetrical mansion.

It was a property of the Oliphants, but passed by marriage to the Arbuthnotts, who held the lands from the 12th century and built the castle. Hugh Arbuthnott was implicated in 1420 for the murder of John Melville of Glenbervie – by throwing him in a cauldron of boiling water, then drinking the resultant broth. In 1641 the family were made Viscounts, and they still live at the house. The gardens are open all year, and the house on specified occasions.

Guided tours only. WC. Disabled access to ground floor. Parking. ££.

Gardens open all year, daily 9.00-17.00. House open certain days and by arrangement.
Tel: 01561 320417   Web: www.arbuthnott.co.uk

Ardvreck Castle

[Map: 6; C4] Off A837, 1.5 miles NW of Inchnadamph, Ardvreck, Highland.
(NGR: NC 240236 LR: 15)

In a remote and picturesque situation by Loch Assynt, Ardvreck Castle is a ruinous square keep, with a distinctive round stair-turret which is corbelled out to square at the top. The lands were a property of the MacLeods of Assynt from the 13th century, and they built the present castle about 1490. It was here that in 1650 the Marquis of Montrose took refuge, but he was turned over to the Covenanters, and executed in Edinburgh. The castle was sacked in 1672, and replaced by nearby Calda House, itself burnt out in 1760 and never restored. The castle is said to be haunted by the ghost of a daughter of the house who threw herself from the top of castle when she found herself wed to the Devil; and the apparition of a tall grey-clad man, who is reported to speak to visitors, although only in Gaelic.

Parking Nearby.

Access at all reasonable times – view from exterior.

Argyll's Lodging, Stirling (HS)

[Map: 7; H5] Off A9, Castle Wynd, Stirling. (NGR: NS 793938 LR: 57)

Located in the historic old burgh of Stirling, Argyll's Lodging is a fine and well-preserved 17th-century town house. Gabled blocks with dormer windows surround a courtyard, while one side is enclosed by a wall. Many of the rooms within the lodging have recently been restored and furnished in 17th-century style.

The Lodging was built by Sir William Alexander of Menstrie, 1st Earl of Stirling and Viscount Canada, but passed to the Campbell Earls of Argyll. The 9th Earl, who was executed for treason in 1685 after leading a rising against James VII, stayed here. The lodging is within easy walking distance of Stirling Castle, the Church of the Holy Rood, Cowane's Hospital and Mar's Wark.

Visitor centre with explanatory displays. Gift shop. WC. Disabled access. Car and coach parking. £ (Joint ticket available with Stirling Castle).

Open all year: Apr-Sep, daily 9.30-18.00; Oct-Mar, daily 9.30-17.00, last ticket sold 30 mins before closing; closed 25/26 Dec and 1/2 Jan.
Tel: 01786 431319

Argyll's Lodging, Stirling – see previous page.

Armadale Castle

[Map: 8; E3] Off A881, Armadale, SE of Sleat, Skye. (NGR: NG 640047 LR: 32)

Located in the fertile and wooded lands of Sleat, Armadale Castle was built in 1815 by the architect James Gillespie Graham for the MacDonalds of Sleat. It was then extended in 1855 by David Bryce, although there was an earlier house by the shore and near the youth hostel. The main part of the later mansion has been burned out and remains ruinous.

Some of the outbuildings house the Clan Donald centre and 'The Museum of the Isles'. A library and study centre offer genealogical research, and there is a countryside information service. There are 40 acres of woodland gardens and nature trails, as well as a walled kitchen garden.

Guided tours. Explanatory displays. Gift shops. Licensed restaurant. Tea room. Picnic area. WC. Disabled access. Car and coach parking. Self-catering accommodation available all year. Group concessions. ££.

Open Apr-Oct, daily 9.30-17.30, last entry 30 mins before closing; gardens, restaurant and shop open all year.

Tel: 01471 844305/227   Web: www.clandonald.com

Arniston House

[Map: 9; H6] Off B6372, 2 miles SW of Gorebridge, Arniston, Midlothian. (NGR: NT 326595 LR: 66)

The present house is a symmetrical classical mansion, dating from 1726 and built by William Adam. It replaced an old house or castle, which dated from before 1592 but was demolished when the present mansion was built. The house was altered in 1754 and 1877. A section was gutted because of dry rot, and is undergoing restoration. The house retains fine plasterwork and period furniture, and the garden is in a pleasant country setting.

Arniston was a property of the Sir James Dundas, who was knighted by James VI, and many of the family were lawyers and statesmen.

Guided tours. WC. Disabled access to ground floor and WC. Car and coach parking. £££ (house).

Open Apr-Jun: guided tours on Tue and Wed starting at 14.00 and 15.30; Jul-mid Sep, Mon-Fri and Sun at 14.00 and 15.30; private groups of 10-50 accepted all year by prior arrangement.

Tel: 01875 830515   Web: www.arniston-house.co.uk

Auchindoun Castle (HS)

[Map: 10; D6] Off A941, 2.5 miles S of Dufftown, Auchindoun, Moray. (NGR: NJ 348374 LR: 28)

In a prominent position with excellent views, Auchindoun Castle is a substantial ruinous L-plan tower house, dating from the 15th century. A courtyard, with a round tower, encloses the tower, and ruined ranges of buildings housed a kitchen and brewhouse.

The existing castle was built for John, Earl of Mar, who was murdered by his brother, James III, at Craigmillar Castle. It passed to Robert Cochrane, a master mason, one of James III's favourites. In 1482 he was hanged from Lauder Bridge, and Auchindoun later went to the Gordons. In 1571 a party of Gordons, led by Adam Gordon of Auchindoun, besieged Corgarff Castle. Corgarff was burnt, killing Margaret Campbell, wife of the Master of Forbes, and her family and retainers, totalling some 27 folk as told in the old ballad 'Edom o' Gordon'. Auchindoun, itself, was sacked and torched in 1591 by the Mackintoshes in revenge for the murder of the Bonnie Earl o' Moray at Donibristle by the Marquis of Huntly and Sir Patrick Gordon of Auchindoun. Gordon was later killed in 1594 at the Battle of Glenlivet.

Parking nearby.

Access at all reasonable times: footpath is steep and may be muddy – view from exterior.
Tel: 01667 460232

Ayton Castle

[Map: 11; H6] Off B9635, 2.5 miles SW of Eyemouth, Borders. (NGR: NT 929614 LR: 67)

Near the Eye Water and the border with England (and pronounced 'Eye-ton'), Ayton Castle is a rambling castellated mansion with a profusion of turrets, battlements and towers. It stands on the site of an old castle, which was captured and slighted by the English in 1448, then besieged in 1497, and then held by them during the invasion of Scotland between 1547-50.

The property was held by the Aytons in medieval times; then passed to the Homes, who were forfeited for their part in the Jacobite Rising of 1715; then the Fordyce family in 1765. In 1834 the old castle was burnt to the ground, and a new mansion, designed by James Gillespie Graham, was built in the 1840s for William Mitchell-Innes and then extended by the architect David Bryce in 1860. It passed to the Liddel-Grainger family, whose descendants still occupy it.

Guided tours. Woodlands. Disabled access. Car and coach parking. £.

Open May-Sep, Sat-Sun 14.00-17.00 or by appt.
Tel: 01890 781212/550   Web: www.aytoncastle.co.uk

Balgonie Castle

[Map: 12; G6] Off A911, 6.5 miles NE of Kirkcaldy, Balgonie, Fife. (NGR: NO 313007 LR: 59)

Balgonie Castle consists of a fine 14th-century keep, with a crenellated battlement and corbiestepped gables, within in a courtyard enclosing ranges of buildings, many of which have been restored.

The castle was built by the Sibbalds, who held the property from before 1246, but passed by marriage to Sir Robert Lundie, later Lord High Treasurer of Scotland. James IV visited the castle in 1496, as did Mary, Queen of Scots, in 1565. The property was sold in 1635 to Alexander Leslie, who fought for Gustavus Adolphus of Sweden during the 30 Years War, and was made a Field Marshall. Leslie resisted Cromwell and was imprisoned in the Tower of London. Balgonie was captured and plundered by Rob Roy MacGregor and 200 clansmen in 1716. The castle has been reoccupied and is being restored. The castle has many stories of ghosts including a 'Green Lady'.

Guided tours. Picnic area. Disabled access to ground floor. Car and coach parking. £. Weddings, receptions and events.

Open all year, daily 10.00-17.00, unless hired for a private function: telephoning in advance is advised.
Tel: 01592 750119   Web: www.balgonie-castle.com

Balhousie Castle

[Map: 13; G5] Hay Street, Perth. (NGR: NO 115244 LR: 58)
Balhousie Castle is a large castellated mansion of 1860, designed by David Smart, but incorporates an L-plan tower house, which dates from the 16th century. It was held by the Eviot family until 1478, when it was sold to the Mercers, and passed in 1625 to the Hay Earls of Kinnoul. It was taken over by the army after World War II, and in 1962 became the regimental headquarters and museum of the Black Watch. The museum features pictures, medals, uniforms and other military mementoes, telling the story of the Black Watch from its founding in 1739 to the present day.
Explanatory displays. Audiotours. Gift shop. WC. Car parking.
Open May-Sep Mon-Sat 10.00-16.30; Oct-Apr, Mon-Fri 10.00-15.30; closed 23 Dec-4 Jan; closed last Sat of Jun; other times by appt.
Tel: 0131 310 8530   Web: www.theblackwatch.co.uk/museum/index.html

Ballindalloch Castle

[Map: 14; D5] On A95, 7.5 miles SW of Aberlour, Ballindalloch, Moray. (NGR: NJ 178365 LR: 28)
Ballindalloch Castle is an impressive and attractive Z-plan tower house, dating from the 16th century but altered and extended in later years to form a grand mansion. The oldest part has a round-stair-tower, which rises a storey higher than the main block and is crowned by a square watch-tower. There are fine gardens and grounds.

The story goes that the castle was started at another site, but as quickly as it was built the stones were pulled down, reputedly by fairies. Eventually a voice was heard, recommending that it was built elsewhere, and the present site was chosen.

The lands had passed to the Grants by 1499, but the castle was captured and sacked by the Gordons during a feud, and burned by the Marquis of Montrose after the Battle of Inverlochy in 1645. In the 18th century it passed by marriage to the Macphersons, and is still occupied by the Macpherson-Grants, one of the few castles built and still occupied by the original family.

The castle is said to be haunted by a 'Green Lady', who haunts the dining room, as well as a 'Pink Lady'; and the ghost of General James Grant, who died in 1806, said to ride around in appreciation of his lands.
Many rooms. Large collection of 17th-century Spanish paintings. Audio-visual presentation. Shop. Tea room. WC. Gardens and grounds. Rock garden. Rose garden. River walks. Famous breed of Aberdeen Angus cattle. Disabled access to ground floor and grounds. £££. Golf course.
Open Good Fri-Sep, Sun-Fri 10.30-17.00, closed Sat; other times by appt.
Tel: 01807 500206   Web: www.ballindallochcastle.co.uk

Balmoral Castle

[Map: 15; E6] Off A93, 7 miles W of Ballater, Kincardine and Deeside. (NGR: NO 255952 LR: 44)

Set in the wooded hills of Royal Deeside, Balmoral Castle is a large castellated mansion, dominated by a tall turreted and battlemented tower. It was built for Prince Albert, consort of Queen Victoria, in 1855; and the castle became their holiday home. It had replaced an old tower house; and is still often used by the royal family.

Robert II had a hunting seat here, but by 1390 a stone castle had been built. The lands were held by the Drummonds and the Gordon family, but passed to the Farquharsons of Inverey in 1662, then the Gordons again. In 1852 Prince Albert bought the estate, and three years later had the present mansion built, demolishing the old castle.

Display of carriages. Exhibition of paintings, works of art and Royal Tartans in the Castle Ballroom. Audiovisual presentation. Pony trekking and pony cart rides. Gift shop. Cafe. WC. Disabled access to exhibition, shops, cafe, gardens and WC. Car and coach parking. £££. Holiday cottages available.

Gardens, grounds and exhibitions open mid Apr-Jul 10.00-17.00 (check opening); last recommended admission 16.00.

Tel: 01339 742334   Web: www.balmoralcastle.com

Balvaird Castle (HS)

[Map: 16; G5] Off A912, 7 miles SE of Perth, 4 miles S of Bridge of Earn, Perthshire. (NGR: NO 169118 LR: 58)

In a picturesque position, Balvaird Castle is a fine and well-preserved L-plan tower house, incorporating work from the 15th century. There are the remains of outbuildings in a courtyard.

Balvaird was a Barclay property, but passed by marriage to the Murrays of Tullibardine in 1500, who built the castle. The family were made Viscounts Stormont and Earls of Mansfield, and they moved to Scone Palace. The castle is still owned by the Murrays, but is in the care of Historic Scotland. *Car and coach parking (when open). £.*

View from exterior: interior open to view some days – tel to check.

Tel: 01786 431324

Balvenie Castle (HS)

[Map: 17; D5] Off A941, N of Dufftown, Moray. (NGR: NJ 326409 LR: 28)

In a pleasant and peaceful location, Balvenie Castle is a large ruinous courtyard castle, with a 13th-century curtain wall and deep ditch, a 16th-century L-plan tower house at one corner, and other 15th-century ranges within the courtyard. The original yett still protects the entrance.

The Comyns built the first castle, then called Mortlach. It was destroyed or much reduced by the forces of Robert the Bruce in 1308, after being visited by Edward I four years earlier. Balvenie passed to the Douglases, then to John Stewart, Earl of Atholl, in 1455. Mary, Queen of Scots, visited in 1562. The castle was used by the Marquis of Montrose during his campaign of 1644-5 against the Covenanters, and it was nearby that a Covenanter force, led by Alexander Leslie, defeated a Royalist army in 1649, taking 900 prisoners. Balvenie was held by the Jacobites in 1689, but in 1715 was held against them by the Duffs. It was not occupied after William Duff committed suicide here in 1718, and was unroofed within six years – although a Hanoverian force briefly held it in 1746.

The castle is said to be haunted by a 'White Lady', as well as a groom and two horses and other disturbances.

Explanatory boards. Gift shop. Picnic area. WC. Disabled WC. Car parking. Group concession. £.

Open Apr-Sep, daily 9.30-18.30; Oct-Nov, Mon-Wed & Sat, 9.30-16.30, Thu 9.30-12.30, Sun 14.00-16.30, closed Fri; last ticket sold 30 mins before closing; closed Dec-Mar.

Tel: 01340 820121

Balvenie Castle – see previous page.

Bishop's Palace, Kirkwall (HS)

[Map: 18; A6] On A960, W of Kirkwall, Orkney. (NGR: HY 449108 LR: 6)

Located opposite the splendid St Magnus Cathedral in the capital of the Orkneys, the Bishop's Palace includes work from the 12th century. There is a rectangular block with a taller round tower at one end. The palace was the residence of the Bishops of Orkney from the 12th century, when the islands were held by Norsemen, but was rebuilt by Bishop Reid in 1541-8. King Hakon Hakonson of

Norway died here in 1263 after defeat by the Scots at the Battle of Largs. It stands by the later Earl's Palace, and there are stories of a passageway linking it to the cathedral. A piper is said to have once been sent into the tunnel, but was afterwards never seen again. It is said at times the sounds of his pipes can still be heard. *Explanatory displays. Parking nearby. £. Joint entry ticket for all Orkney monuments available.*

Open Apr-Sep, daily 9.30-18.30; Oct-Nov, Mon-Wed & Sat, 9.30-16.30, Thu 9.30-12.30, Sun 14.00-16.30, closed Fri; closed Dec-Mar; last ticket 30 mins before closing.

Tel: 01856 871918

Blackness Castle (HS)

[Map: 19; H5] Off B903 or B9109, 4 miles NE of Linlithgow, 4 miles E of Bo'ness, Falkirk. (NGR: NT 056803 LR: 65)

An impressive and somewhat foreboding place, Blackness is built on a promontory in the Firth of Forth and is a strong castle

Blackness Castle

which is ranged around a courtyard. The oldest part is the tall central keep, which dates from the 15th century, but the stronghold was greatly altered and strengthened for artillery in later years.

In medieval times Blackness was an important port for the royal burgh of Linlithgow. The castle is first mentioned in 1449 as a prison and was probably built by the Crichtons, but it was burned by an English fleet in 1481. Cardinal Beaton was imprisoned here in 1543. When Mary, Queen of Scots, fled to England in 1568, the castle held out for her until 1573. It was captured in 1650 during Cromwell's invasion, being bombarded from land and sea.

In the 19th century Blackness was greatly altered to hold powder and stores, and became the central ammunition depot for Scotland.

Gift shop. Refreshments. WC. Picnic area. Parking. £.

Open all year: Apr-Sep, daily 9.30-18.30; Oct-Mar, Sat-Wed 9.30-16.30, closed Thu & Fri; closed 25/26 Dec and 1/2 Jan.

Tel: 01506 834807

Blair Castle

[Map: 20; F5] Off B8079, 7 miles N of Pitlochry, 1 mile NW of Blair Atholl, Perthshire.
(NGR: NN 867662 LR: 43)

White-washed and castellated and standing in its own parkland, Blair Castle is a rambling mansion of the Dukes of Atholl, and incorporates the 13th-century Comyn's Tower. The building had been completely altered and lowered in the 18th century to turn it into a plain mansion, but was remodelled and recast in 1872 by the architect David Bryce on the instructions of the 3rd Duke. It has fine Georgian plasterwork and the castle houses many Jacobite mementoes. There is a walled garden and fine grounds.

In 1263 the Comyns held the castle, and Edward III of England stayed here in 1336. James V visited in 1529, as did Mary, Queen of Scots, in 1564, by which time it had passed to the Earls of Atholl. The lands passed, along with the titles, to the Murrays in 1629; and in 1653 the castle was besieged, captured and partly destroyed with gunpowder by Cromwell. It was sufficiently complete, however, to be garrisoned by Viscount or 'Bonnie' Dundee, John Graham of Claverhouse, in 1689, and it was here that his body was brought after the Battle of Killiecrankie.

The Earls of Atholl were made Marquises, then Dukes of Atholl in 1703. Bonnie Prince Charlie stayed here in 1745. The following year the castle was held by Hanoverian forces, and attacked and damaged by one of the Duke of Atholl's family, Lord George Murray, Bonnie Prince Charlie's general, although he failed to capture it. Blair was the last castle in Britain to be besieged.

The Duke of Atholl has the unique distinction of having the only remaining private army in Europe. Robert Burns visited in 1787; and Queen Victoria also visited the castle.

Some 30 interesting rooms. Collections of paintings, tapestries, arms, armour, china, costumes and Jacobite mementoes. Fine Georgian plasterwork. Guided tours for groups. Gift shop. Licensed restaurant. Sun terrace. Walled garden. Picnic area. Deer park. Pony trekking. Play area. Disabled access to ground floor & facilities. Car and coach parking. Group concessions. £££. Weddings and functions.

Open Apr-end Oct, daily 10.00-18.00; last entry 90 mins before closing; also on Tue and Sat, Nov-Dec.

Tel: 01796 481207   Web: www.blair-castle.co.uk

Blairquhan

[Map: 21; I4] Off B7045, 7 miles SE of Maybole, Ayrshire – signposted from A77.
(NGR: NS 367055 LR: 70)

Blairquhan is a large castellated mansion, which was designed by William Burn in 1821-4. It replaced a courtyard house incorporating the 14th-century McWhurter's Tower and a range from 1573. There is a walled garden.

Bothwell Castle

It was a property of the MacWhurters, but passed to the Kennedys, then the Whitefoords in 1623. Charles Whitefoord of Blairquhan fought for the Hanoverians at the Battle of Culloden in 1746. It was acquired by the Hunter Blairs in 1790, and is still held by the same family.

Self-guided tours – guided tours by arrangement. Gift shop. Tea room. WC. Walled garden. Picnic area. Partial disabled access and WC. Car and coach parking. £££. Available for weddings, corporate events, etc; holiday cottages in grounds.

Open mid Jul-mid Aug, daily 13.30-17.00, closed Mon; last entry 45 mins before closing; check exact dates with castle; grounds open until 18.00.

Tel: 01655 770239   Web: www.blairquhan.co.uk

Bothwell Castle (HS)

[Map: 22; H5] Off B7071 at Uddingston, 3 miles NW of Hamilton, Lanarkshire.
(NGR: NS 688594 LR: 64)

In a fine location above the Clyde, Bothwell Castle is one of the largest and most impressive early stone castles in Scotland. A once magnificent ruinous round keep stands at one side of a walled courtyard, the walls of which rise to 60 feet and enclose the remains of other buildings. The round keep, protected by a ditch, was partly destroyed in the 14th century, but is of particularly fine workmanship.

Bothwell Castle was of major importance during the Wars of Independence, and was a property of the Murrays. It was held by the English in 1298-9, but was besieged by the Scots and eventually taken after 14 months. In 1301 Edward I recaptured the castle, and it became the headquarters of the English administration. It was surrendered to the Scots in 1314 after the Battle of Bannockburn, and the keep was partly demolished at this time.

In 1336 the castle was taken and rebuilt by the English, and Edward III made Bothwell his headquarters, but it was slighted again after recapture by the Scots around 1337. The castle was rebuilt by the Earls of Douglas in the 1360s, but was partly dismantled for materials in the 17th century.

Exhibition. Explanatory boards. Gift shop. Refreshments. WC. Car and coach parking. £.

Open all year: Apr-Sep, daily 9.30-18.30; Oct-Mar, Sat-Wed 9.30-16.30, closed Thu & Fri; closed 25/26 Dec and 1/2 Jan.

Tel: 01698 816894

Bowhill

[Map: 23; H6] Off A708, 3 miles W of Selkirk, Borders
(NGR: NT 426278 LR: 73)

Home of the Duke and Duchess of Buccleuch, Bowhill is an extensive rambling mansion, dating mainly from 1812, although part may date from early in the previous century. There may have been a castle or an old house at the site; and the house was remodelled in 1831-2 by the architect William Burn. There are fine collections of paintings and artefacts, including the Duke of Monmouth's saddle and execution shirt. The ruins of Newark Castle are in the grounds.

Fine collections of paintings and artefacts, including the Duke of Monmouth's saddle and execution shirt. Audio-visual presentation. Restored Victorian kitchen and fire engine display. Sales area (gift shop Jul). Restaurant. WC. Garden and country park. Disabled facilities; wheelchair visitors free. Ruins of Newark Castle in grounds. Car and coach parking. ££.

Park open Easter-end Aug; house open Jun, Thu & Sun, 13.00-16.00; Jul, daily 13.00-17.00; Aug, Tue & Thu 13.00-16.00; tel to confirm; other times by appt for educational groups.

Tel: 01750 22204   Web: www.heritageontheweb.co.uk

Braemar Castle

[Map: 24; E5] On A93, 0.5 miles NE of Braemar, Kincardine and Deeside. (NGR: NO 156924 LR: 43)

In a fine, mountainous location, Braemar Castle is an altered 17th-century L-plan tower house, with battlemented turrets crowning the corners. It is defended by an 18th-century star-shaped artillery defence. There is an unventilated pit-prison, and the original iron yett.

The castle was built in 1628 by John Erskine, 2nd Earl of Mar. It was captured and torched by Jacobites under Farquharson of Inverey in 1689, although it had held out against John Graham of Claverhouse. 'Bobbing John', the 6th Earl of Mar, led the 1715 Jacobite Rising, but after its failure fled to France. The castle remained ruinous but passed to the Farquharsons; and in 1748 was leased by the government, and turned into a barracks. The Farquharsons restored and reoccupied the castle in the early 19th century, and Queen Victoria visited when she attended the Braemar Gathering.

The castle is said to be haunted by the blonde-haired phantom of a young bride, who is said to have thrown herself from the battlements believing she had been abandoned by her husband. Another ghost is reportedly that of John Farquharson of Inverey, also known as the 'Black Colonel', who burnt the place in 1689.

Many interesting rooms. Guided tours. Explanatory sheets. Gift shop. Refreshments. WC. Picnic area. Car and coach parking. Group concessions. £.

Open Apr-Oct, Sat-Thu, 10.00-18.00, closed Fri; Jul-Aug, daily 10.00-18.00; last entry 30 mins before closing.

Tel: 01339 741219   Web: www.braemarcastle.co.uk

Brodick Castle (NTS)

[Map: 25; H3] Off A841, 1.5 miles N of Brodick, Cladach, Arran. (NGR: NS 016378 LR: 69)

Built on a prominent site above Brodick Bay, the castle was developed out of a 15th-century keep, the lower part of which may date from 200 years or so earlier. The building was extended and remodelled down the centuries, and extensive baronial additions were made in 1844 by the architect James Gillespie Graham. There are extensive gardens and grounds, and access to Goatfell, the highest hill on Arran.

Arran was held by the Norsemen and the property only passed to the Scottish Crown in 1266. The castle was held by the English during the Wars of Independence until 1307 when recaptured by the Scots, perhaps led by Robert the Bruce. It was damaged by English ships in 1406, and by the MacDonald Lord of the Isles about 1455. Arran passed to the Boyds in 1467, then to the Hamiltons in 1503. The 1st Hamilton Earl of Arran rebuilt the castle soon afterwards, but it was damaged in a raid in 1528, and again in 1544 by the Earl of Lennox for Henry VIII of England.

It was extended and remodelled by the 2nd Earl of Arran, Regent to Mary, Queen of Scots, in the

Brodie Castle

1550s, but was captured by the Campbells in 1639 to be retaken by the Hamiltons. In the 1650s the castle was occupied by Cromwell's troops. Extensive additions were made for the marriage of Princess Marie of Baden to the 11th Duke of Hamilton. In 1958 Brodick was taken over by The National Trust for Scotland. The castle is said to be haunted by a 'Grey Lady', perhaps the ghost of a lady starved to death in the dungeons because she had plague, perhaps a poor lass who committed suicide after becoming pregnant. There are also stories of a White Deer, reportedly seen when one of the family is near death.

Collections of furniture, porcelain, pictures and silver. Gift shop. Licensed restaurant. WC. Gardens and country park, ice house, summer house and adventure playground. Nature trail and access to Goatfell. Disabled WC and access. Car and coach parking. £££

Castle, restaurant and walled garden open Easter-Oct, daily 11.00-17.00, last entry 60 mins before closing; reception centre and shop also open 1 Nov-22 Dec; country park open all year, daily 9.00-sunset.

Tel: 01770 302202

Brodie Castle (NTS)

[Map: 26; D5] Off A96, 4.5 miles W of Forres, Brodie, Moray. (NGR: NH 980578 LR: 27)

A large and impressive building, Brodie Castle consists of a substantial 16th-century Z-plan tower house, with extensive additions, which was further enlarged in the 19th century by the architect William Burn.

   The property was owned by the Brodies from 1160. It was burnt in 1645 because the Brodies were Covenanters, although much of the internal work survived; and was damaged by fire again in 1786. The house was renovated in 1980 after passing to The National Trust for Scotland, although it is still occupied by the Brodies. There are gardens and grounds, and a fine Pictish carved cross-slab by the avenue up to the castle. The building is said to be haunted by the apparition of a woman, believed by some to be the ghost of Lady Margaret Duff, who was burned to death in 1786.

Collection of paintings and furniture. Guided tours available. Explanatory displays. Gift shop. Tearoom. WC. Picnic area. Garden and adventure playground. Disabled facilities including Braille guides. Car and coach parking. Group concessions. £££

Open Easter-Jun, Sun-Thu 12.00-16.00; Jul-Sep, daily 12.00-16.00; grounds open all year, daily 9.30-sunset.

Tel: 01309 641371

Brodie Castle – see previous page.

Broughton House, Kirkcudbright (NTS)

[Map: 27; J4] Off A711 or A755, 12 High Street, Kirkcudbright, Dumfries and Galloway.
(NGR: NX 682511 LR: 83)

Situated in the picturesque town of Kirkcudbright, Broughton House, which dates from the 17th-century or earlier, was a town house of the Murrays of Broughton. It was later the home and studio of the artist E. A. Hornel, one of the 'Glasgow Boys', and he stayed here from 1901-33 . It contains many of his works, along with other paintings by contemporary artists, as well as rare Scottish books, including valuable editions of the work of Robert Burns. There is a Japanese-style garden, laid out by Hornel, leading down to River Dee estuary.

Explanatory displays. Garden. WC. Car parking. Group concessions. £.
Open Easter-Oct, daily 12.00-17.00; Jul-Aug, 10.00-17.00.
Tel: 01557 330437

Broughty Castle

[Map: 28; G6] Off A930, 4 miles E of Dundee, S of Broughty Ferry, Angus. (NGR: NO 465304 LR: 54)

Standing by the sea guarding the northern part of the Firth of Tay, Broughty Castle is a tall 15th-century keep of five storeys, with a later wing and artillery emplacements. There are fine views.

The Grays of Fowlis built the original castle in the 1490s. Patrick, 4th Lord Gray, a treacherous fellow, delivered up Broughty Castle to the English around 1547, who then raided much of the surrounding countryside. The castle was stormed by the Scots with French help three years later, and was partly demolished. It was taken by Cromwell's forces in 1651, and Alexander Leslie, Earl of Leven, was imprisoned here. It passed to the Fotheringham family in 1666.

Although ruinous by 1820, it was bought by the government in the next decades, and restored and given gun emplacements. The castle now houses a museum of whaling and fishery, arms and armour, and local history. There are fine views of the Tay.

Explanatory displays. Sales area. Refreshments. WC. No wheelchair access. Parking.
Open Apr-Sep, Mon-Sat 10.00-16.00, Sun 12.30-16.00; Oct-Mar, Tue-Sat 10.00-16.00, Sun 12.30-16.00, closed Mon.
Tel: 01382 436916   Web: www.dundeecity.gov.uk

Burleigh Castle (HS)

[Map: 29; G5] On A911, 1.5 miles N of Kinross, Perthshire. (NGR: NO 130046 LR: 58)

Although once a larger and more imposing stronghold, Burleigh Castle now consists of a ruined 15th-century keep, a section of courtyard wall with a gate, and a round corner tower. The tower is corbelled out to square for its upper chamber.

It was a property of the Balfours of Burleigh, and was visited by James IV. In 1707 the Master of Burleigh fell in love with a young servant girl, and was sent abroad to forget her. He swore if she married, he would return and kill her husband. She married Henry Stenhouse, the schoolmaster of Inverkeithing, and the Master duly returned, then shot and killed the poor man. Burleigh fled, but in 1709 was captured, tried and sentenced to death by the axe. However, he managed to escape by changing clothes with his sister, and fled to the continent. He returned and fought for the Jacobites in the 1715 Rising, after which the family were forfeited. Burleigh died unmarried in 1757.
Parking nearby.
Access at all reasonable times: keys available locally.

Cadzow Castle (HS)

[Map: 30; H5] Off A72, 1.5 miles SE of Hamilton, Lanarkshire. (NGR: NS 734538 LR: 64)

Standing in the fine policies of Chatelherault Park, Cadzow Castle is now very ruinous, but dates from the 12th century. Most of the present ruin consists of a tower house of 1540, with outbuildings and a courtyard. It is an early example of a castle built to withstand artillery.

The castle was used by the kings of Scots, including David I, but passed to the Comyns, then to the Hamiltons. The Hamiltons were made Dukes of Chatelherault in France — a title granted by Henri II. Mary, Queen of Scots, visited the castle in 1568 after escaping from Lochleven Castle. The castle was besieged two years later, and the castle surrendered after two days. In 1579 the castle was seized by the Regent Morton's forces, and was dismantled to be left as a ruin.

The castle is currently being consolidated by Historic Scotland and can be viewed from the exterior.
Park open to the public except Christmas and New Year – castle: view from exterior.
Tel: 01698 426213

Caerlaverock Castle (HS)

*[Map: 31; J5] Off B725, 7 miles SE of Dumfries, Caerlaverock, Dumfries and Galloway.
(NGR: NY 026656 LR: 84)*

Once a formidable fortress and still a fantastic ruin, Caerlaverock Castle is a very picturesque place, and is built around a triangular courtyard which is defended by a water-filled moat. There is a gatehouse at one side, round towers at two corners, and ranges of buildings in between.

The castle was built in the 13th century by the Maxwells, but was captured by Edward I of England in 1300 after a siege, although it was eventually retaken by the Scots after many battles. Murdoch Stewart, son of Robert Duke of Albany, was imprisoned in the castle before being executed in 1425: and gave the name to 'Murdoch's Tower'.

James V visited the castle prior to defeat at Solway Moss in 1542. The castle was surrendered to the English three years later, but was recaptured by the Scots. In 1640 Caerlaverock was taken by a force of Covenanters after a siege of 13 weeks, and then partly dismantled. The castle was then abandoned.

Visitor centre, children's park and nature trail to old castle. Shop. Tea room. Picnic area. Explanatory panels. Replica siege engine. Reasonable disabled access and WC. Car and coach parking. Group concessions. £.

Open all year: Apr-Sep, daily 9.30-18.30; Oct-Mar, daily 9.30-16.30; last ticket 30 mins before closing; closed 25/26 Dec and 1/2 Jan.

Tel: 01387 770244

Caisteal Bharraich

[Map: 32; B4] Off A838, 1 mile W of Tongue, Sutherland, Highland. (NGR: NC 581567   LR: 10)
Caisteal Bharraich, built on a promontory with fine views along the Kyle of Tongue, is a two-storey ruined tower house of the Bishops of Caithness, then the Mackays. The basement was vaulted. The castle can be reached by a steep path from the gate beside the Royal Bank of Scotland.
Parking nearby.
Access at all reasonable times: long walk and care should be taken.

Caisteal Maol

[Map: 33; E3] Off A850, 0.5 miles E of Kyleakin, Skye. (NGR: NG 758264   LR: 33)
Overlooking the old ferry crossing and the new bridge between Skye and the mainland at Kyle of Lochalsh, Caisteal Maol, 'the bare castle', is a very ruinous 15th-century keep.

The castle was traditionally built by a Norse princess called 'Saucy Mary' who was married to a MacKinnon chief. Their main income was from tolls on ships sailing through the narrow passage at Kyle. King Hakon of Norway stopped here on his way south in 1263 to eventual defeat at the Battle of Largs, but he gave the castle its older name: Dunakin or Dun Hakon.

It was a stronghold of the MacKinnons of Strath or Strathordil. The MacKinnons fought for the Marquis of Montrose at both Auldearn and Inverlochy in 1645, a MacKinnon regiment fought for Charles II at Worcester, and they were Jacobites, fighting at the Battle of Sheriffmuir in 1715 and Glenshiel in 1719. The Chief of MacKinnon sheltered Bonnie Prince Charlie, after his defeat at Culloden in 1746, for which he was given the recipe for Drambuie, a whisky liqueur.
Access at all reasonable times.

Callendar House

[Map: 34; H5] Off A803, Callendar Park, in Falkirk. (NGR: NS 898794   LR: 65)
Set in an extensive country park with woodland walks and a boating pond, Callendar House, a large ornate mansion of the 1870s with towers and turrets, incorporates a 14th- or 15th-century castle. The castle once had a deep ditch and courtyard, and still has very thick walls. The building was greatly altered and extended in later centuries, and is an imposing edifice.

It was held by the Livingstone family from 1345, who were made Earls of Callendar in 1641, and then of Linlithgow. Mary, Queen of Scots, stayed here several times in the 1560s. The castle was stormed and captured by Cromwell in 1650s. The Livingstones were forfeited for their part in the 1715 Jacobite Rising, and the house was leased to the Boyd Earl of Kilmarnock, although he was himself beheaded for his part in the 1745 Rising. Bonnie Prince Charlie stayed here the same year;

Cardoness Castle

and General Hawley and a Hanoverian army camped here before going on to defeat at the nearby Battle of Falkirk the following year. The house passed to William Forbes, a copper merchant, and he and his descendants remodelled and extended the house. The family held the property until the 20th century, but it is now in the care of the local council.

The house features the Roman finds, a reconstruction of an 1820s clockmaker, printer and general store, a Georgian working kitchen, history research centre, displays on 'William Forbes's Falkirk' and temporary exhibitions.

Permanent displays. Temporary exhibitions. Restored 1820s kitchen with costumed interpretation. History research centre. Contemporary art gallery. Gift shop. Tea room. Garden. Park with boating, pitch and putt. Woodland walks. Children's play area. WC. Disabled access. Car and coach parking. Group concessions. £.

Open all year: Mon-Sat 10.00-17.00; also Apr-Sep, Sun 14.00-17.00; open most public hols; park open all year.

Tel: 01324 503770   Web: www.falkirk.gov.uk/cultural/

Cardoness Castle (HS)

[Map: 35; J4] Off A75, 1 mile SW of Gatehouse of Fleet, Dumfries and Galloway.
(NGR: NX 591552 LR: 83)

Standing on a rocky mound above the Water of Fleet, Cardoness Castle is a ruinous and somewhat stark rectangular keep, dating from the second half of the 15th century, with a courtyard which enclosed outbuildings. There are fine fireplaces as well as excellent views.

Cardoness passed to the MacCullochs by marriage around 1450. They were an unruly lot, the 2nd MacCulloch laird being outlawed in 1471 and again in 1480. His successor, Ninian, robbed the widow of the 2nd laird of all her goods. Thomas MacCulloch, his son, besieged the Adairs of Dunskey in 1489, and then plundered the castle of his kinsman, MacCulloch of Adair. Thomas died at the Battle of Flodden in 1513. The last of the family was Sir Godfrey MacCulloch, who shot William Gordon of Buck (or Bush) o' Bield in 1690, fled abroad, returned and was spotted in a church in Edinburgh. He was beheaded in 1697 by the Maiden, an early Scottish guillotine preserved in the Museum of Scotland in Edinburgh. Cardoness had passed to the Gordons in 1629, then to the Maxwells.

Visitor centre. Exhibition and scale model of the castle. Shop. Picnic area. WC. Car and coach parking. Group concessions. £.

Open Apr-Sep, Mon-Sun 9.30-18.30; Oct, Sat-Wed 9.30-16.30, closed Thu-Fri; Nov-Mar wknds only, 9.30-16.30; last ticket 30 mins before closing; closed 25/26 Dec and 1/2 Jan.

Tel: 01557 814427

Carleton Castle

[Map: 36; I4] Off A77, 6 miles SW of Girvan, Lendalfoot, Ayrshire. (NGR: NX 133895 LR: 76)

Standing above the sea, Carleton Castle is a ruinous rectangular keep, dating from the 15th century, and long a property of the Cathcart family.

This was the home of Sir John Cathcart. The story goes that he married several women in turn, after having murdered the last, presumably to acquire their dowries. He was eventually wedded to May Kennedy of Culzean but, realizing what was going to happen, she managed to push Cathcart to his death from cliffs. It is said that ghostly cries and screams have been heard from the castle.
Parking nearby.

Access at all reasonable times – care should be taken.

Carnasserie Castle (HS)

[Map: 37; G3] Off A816, 8.5 miles N of Lochgilphead, 1 mile N of Kilmartin, Argyll.
(NGR: NM 837009 LR: 55)

Lying in a brooding spot above the road, Carnasserie Castle is a ruinous 16th-century tower house and lower hall-block. The tower rises to five storeys and the walls are pierced by gunloops and shot-holes.

It was built by John Carswell, who published the first ever book in Gaelic in 1567, the Gaelic version of the Book of Common Order. He was Rector (or Parson) of Kilmartin, then Chancellor of

the Chapel-Royal at Stirling. He was made Bishop of Argyll and the Isles in 1566 by Mary, Queen of Scots, after the Reformation. On his death in 1572, Carnasserie passed to the Campbells of Auchinbreck, and it was captured and sacked by the MacLeans and MacLachlans during the Campbell Earl of Argyll's rebellion of 1685.
Picnic area. Car and coach parking.

Access at all reasonable times.

Carrick House

[Map: 38; A6] Off B9063, Carrick, N of Eday, Orkney. (NGR: HY 567384 LR: 5)

Located on the tranquil and picturesque island of Eday, Carrick House, a 17th-century harled and corbiestepped house of two storeys and an attic, may incorporate part of an older building. An arched entrance to the courtyard is dated 1633, although the house was extended in later years.

Carsluith Castle

It was built by John Stewart, Earl of Carrick, younger brother of the notorious Patrick Stewart, Earl of Orkney, but passed on his death to the Buchanans, then to James Fea of Clestrain, who captured the pirate John Gow in 1725. Gow, born in Stromness in Orkney, was not a very successful pirate and managed to run his ship aground on the Calf of Eday. He was caught and executed. The island passed in 1848 to the Hebden family who still occupy Carrick House.

Guided tours take in the house, garden and other parts of the island. There are spectacular views.
Guided tours. Picnic area. WC. Limited disabled access. Car parking. £.
Open Jun-Sep, Sun 14.00 onwards – tel to check; other times by arrangement.
Tel: 01857 622260   Web: www.eday.orkney.sch.uk/tourism/carricktour/index.htm

Carsluith Castle (HS)

[Map: 39; J4] On A75, 6/5 miles SW of Gatehouse of Fleet, Carsluith, Dumfries and Galloway.
(NGR: NX 495542 LR: 83)
Carsluith Castle is a rectangular 15th-century keep, to which was added a taller stair-wing in the 16th century, making the castle L-plan. The tower is dated 1586.

Carsluith was held by the Cairns family, but in 1460 passed to James Lindsay, Chamberlain of Galloway and probable builder of the keep, then by marriage to Richard Brown. Gilbert Brown of Carsluith was the last abbot of Sweetheart Abbey and a noted supporter of the Catholic side in the Reformation. In 1605 he was imprisoned in Blackness Castle, then he was later exiled to France, where he died seven years later. The Browns went to India in 1748, and abandoned the castle.
Parking nearby.

Castle Campbell (HS)

[Map: 40; G5] Off A91, 12 miles E of Stirling, 0.5 miles N of Dollar, Clackmannan.
(NGR: NS 962994 LR: 58)
An impressive and picturesque ruin in a wonderful location, Castle Campbell was built where the Burns of Care and Sorrow join, overlooked by Gloom Hill, and was originally known as Castle Gloom. A large and strong 15th-century keep, altered in later centuries, stands at one corner of a substantial ruinous courtyard, enclosed by a curtain wall. There is an unusual arched loggia, and spectacular views.

It was a property of the Stewarts, but passed by marriage to Colin Campbell, 1st Earl of Argyll and Chancellor of Scotland, and he had the name changed to Castle Campbell in 1489. John Knox visited

in 1566. The Marquis of Montrose failed to take the castle in 1645, although he ravaged the lands. Cromwell's forces occupied the castle in 1653, and only part was restored after being torched the following year. The Ogilvies are also said to have burnt the castle after the Campbells had destroyed their own stronghold of Airlie.

Gift shop. Tearoom. WC. Car parking. Group concessions. £. Owned by NTS but administered by Historic Scotland.

Open all year: Apr-Sep, daily 9.30-18.30; Oct-Mar, Sat-Wed 9.30-16.30, closed Thu & Fri; last ticket 30 mins before closing; closed 25/26 Dec and 1/2 Jan.
Tel: 01259 742408

Castle Fraser (NTS)

[Map: 41; E6] Off B993 or B977, 6.5 miles SW of Inverurie, Aberdeenshire. (NGR: NJ 724126 LR: 38)
A splendid and well-preserved building, Castle Fraser is a tall and massive Z-plan tower house, mostly dating from between 1575 and 1636. Two projecting wings form a courtyard, the final side being

completed by other buildings, one with an arched gateway. There is a walled garden.

The property was acquired by the Frasers in 1454, in 1633 they were made Lords Fraser, and built the castle. The Frasers were Covenanters, and their lands were ravaged in 1638, and then again six years later by Montrose. The Frasers were later Jacobites, and the 4th Lord died a fugitive following the 1715 Rising after falling from a cliff. The property remained with the Frasers until 1921, but is now cared for by The National Trust for Scotland.

Explanatory sheets. Many interesting rooms. Gift shop. Tea room. Picnic area. Garden and grounds. Walled garden. Adventure playground. Car and coach parking. Group concessions. £££.
Open Easter-Sep: April-Jun & Sep, Tue-Thu & Sat-Sun, 12.00-17.00, last 45 mins before closing, closed Mon & Fri; Jul-Aug, daily 11.00-17.00.
Tel: 01330 833463

Castle Kennedy

[Map: 42; J4] Off A75, 3 miles E of Stranraer, Dumfries and Galloway.
(NGR: NX 111609 LR: 82)
Set among fine gardens and originally on an island in a loch, Castle Kennedy is a large ruinous 17th-century E-plan tower house. The existing castle was started in 1607 by John Kennedy, 5th Earl of

Cassillis, and replaced an older stronghold. The property passed to the Dalrymples of Stair around 1677. A fire gutted the castle in 1716, and it was never restored. Lochinch Castle, an elegant modern mansion, stands nearby.

The 75 acres of gardens are laid out between two lochs originally in 1730, with impressive terraces and avenues around a large lily pond. The gardens are famous for rhododendrons, azaleas, emborthriums and many other specimen plants. There is a walled garden.

Gift shop. Tea room. Plant centre. Disabled access: admission free to disabled visitors. Disabled access. Car and coach parking. £

Lochinch Castle not open to the public; gardens open Apr-Sep, daily 10.00-17.00.

Tel: 01776 702024   Web: www.castlekennedygardens.co.uk

Castle Menzies

[Map: 43; G5] Off B846, 1.5 miles NW of Aberfeldy, Castle Menzies, Perthshire.
(NGR: NN 837496 LR: 52)

In a picturesque location, Castle Menzies is a fine altered and extended 16th-century tower house, consisting of a main block and two taller square towers, projecting at opposite corners. Many turrets crown the building. An extension was added by the architect William Burn in 1840; and there is some fine wooden panelling.

It was a property of the Menzies family, and built after an older stronghold, known as Place of Weem, was torched. The castle was occupied by Cromwell's forces in the 1650s, and was captured by Jacobites in 1715. Bonnie Prince Charlie stayed here for two nights in 1746, but four days later the castle was seized by Hanoverian forces, led by the Duke of Cumberland. The chiefs did not support the Jacobite Risings, although many of the clan were killed at Culloden in 1746 fighting for Bonnie Prince Charlie. The clan held the property until 1918 when it was lost, although it was bought back by the Menzies Clan Society in 1957. A small museum about the clan has interesting exhibits including Bonnie Prince Charlie's death mask.

Access to all the old part of the castle. Explanatory displays. Museum about Menzies Clan. Gift shop. Tea room. Disabled access to part of ground floor, tea room and gift shop. WC. Disabled access. Car and limited coach parking. Group concessions. £

Open Apr or Easter-mid Oct, Mon-Sat 10.30-17.00, Sun 14.00-17.00; last entry 30 mins before closing.

Tel: 01887 820982

Castle Roy

[Map: 44; E5] On B970, 3 miles SW of Grantown on Spey, Highland. (NGR: NJ 007219 LR: 36)

Castle Roy, the name coming from the Gaelic 'Caisteal Ruadh' meaning 'Red Castle', is a ruinous courtyard castle, rectangular in plan and with a square tower at one corner. It was built by the Comyns in the 13th century.

Explanatory board. Parking.

Access at all reasonable times.

Castle Stalker

[Map: 45; G3] Off A828, 20 miles N of Oban, Portnacroish, Argyll. (NGR: NM 921473 LR: 49)

Standing dramatically on a small island in a magnificent location at the mouth of Loch Laich, Castle Stalker is a tall, massive and simple keep. It was built by Duncan Stewart of Appin, who was made Chamberlain of the Isles, and is believed to have been used by James IV as a hunting lodge. In 1620 the castle was sold to the Campbells, although only after some double dealing, but the Stewarts retrieved it after a long siege in 1685. The garrison, however, surrendered to William and Mary's forces in 1690. In 1715 the clan fought for the Jacobites at Sheriffmuir during the Jacobite Rising.

The 9th Chief did not support the 1745 Rising – the clan were led by Stewart of Ardshiel – and the lands were sold in 1765. The castle was abandoned about 1780, but restored from ruin in the 1960s. *Parking nearby. Not suitable for coach parties. £££.*
Open for some days in the summer.
Tel: 01883 622768   Web: www.castlestalker.com

Castle Sween (HS)

[Map: 46; H3] Off B8025, 11 miles SE of Lochgilphead, E shore of Loch Sween, Argyll.
(NGR: NR 712789 LR: 62)
Standing in a beautiful spot on a rocky ridge on the shore of Loch Sween, Castle Sween is an impressive courtyard castle, dating from the 11th or 12th century. It consists of a curtain wall, enclosing a

rectangular courtyard, and a strong 15th-century keep.
   One of the earliest castles in Scotland, it was built at a time when this part of Scotland was still under Norse rule, and is said to be named after Sueno, an 11th-century Dane. The castle was held by the MacSweens, until captured by Robert the Bruce in 1315; then the MacMillans; the Stewarts of Menteith; then the MacNeils of Gigha for the MacDonald Lord of the Isles until in 1481 when the Campbells became keepers for the Crown. The castle was captured and partly dismantled by Alaisdair Colkitto MacDonald in 1647. One tower collapsed in the 19th century, but the castle has since been consolidated.
Parking nearby.
Access at all reasonable times.

Castle of Mey

[Map: 47; B5] Off A836, 7 miles N of Castletown, Castle of Mey, Caithness. (NGR: ND 290739 LR: 12)
In the far north of Scotland, Castle of Mey is an altered Z-plan tower house, dating from the 16th century, with a main block of three storeys and an attic, and higher towers at opposite corners. It was remodelled in the 18th century, then again in 1819 by William Burn, and also in 1957. There is a walled garden.
   The lands originally belonged to the Bishop of Caithness, but in 1566 were acquired by the Sinclair Earls of Caithness, who built the castle. The 6th Earl bankrupted the family, and the earldom was claimed by the Campbells, although this was disputed by Sinclair of Keiss. The Sinclairs eventually

Castle of Old Wick

recovered the earldom and castle, although only after a protracted dispute and much bloodshed. In 1952 the castle was sold to Elizabeth Bowes Lyon, the Queen Mother, who had it restored. She died in 2002.

The castle is said to be haunted by the ghost of a daughter of the 5th Earl. She fell in love with a ploughman, and her father had her imprisoned in one of the attic rooms. She threw herself from one of the windows, and her sad spectre, a 'Green Lady', reportedly haunts the castle.

Disabled access restricted to principal floor. £££.

Open to the public in the summer: check with castle or on website.

Tel: 01847 851473   Web: www.castleofmey.org.uk

Castle of Old Wick (HS)

[Map: 48; C6] Off A9, 1 mile S of Wick, Castle of Old Wick, Caithness. (NGR: ND 369488 LR: 12)

One of the oldest castles in Scotland, Castle of Old Wick consists of a simple square keep standing on a promontory on cliffs above the sea, cut off by a ditch. It stands in a prominent position with fine views.

It was built in the 12th century when this part of Scotland was ruled from Orkney by the Norsemen, possibly by Harold Maddadson, Earl of Caithness, who was blinded and castrated by Alexander II. It was a property of the Cheynes in the 14th century, then the Oliphants, before passing to the Sutherland Lord Duffus. In 1569, during a feud with the Sinclairs, the castle was besieged, starved into submission, and captured by John Sinclair, Master of Caithness. It was sold to the Sinclairs in 1606, but later passed to the Dunbars of Hempriggs.

Parking nearby.

Access at all reasonable times - great care must be taken.

Tel: 01667 460232

Castle of St John, Stranraer

[Map: 49; J3] Off A77, in centre of Stranraer, Dumfries and Galloway. (NGR: NX 061608 LR: 82)

Castle of St John or Stranraer Castle is an altered 16th-century L-plan tower house, which rises to three storeys and has a corbelled-out parapet. A further storey has been added above parapet level.

It was probably built by Adair of Kilhilt around 1511, although it may be older. The castle passed to the Kennedys of Chappel before 1596, then to the Dalrymples of Stair in 1680. John Graham of Claverhouse, 'Bonnie Dundee' or 'Bloody Clavers', stayed here while suppressing Covenanters from 1682-5 as one of his duties as the Sheriff of Galloway. The castle is now a museum, with exhibitions charting the history from its building through Covenanting times to its use as a town jail in the 19th century

Explanatory displays and videos. Gift shop. Family activities. Parking nearby. £.

Open Easter-mid Sep, Mon-Sat 10.00-13.00 and 14.00-17.00; closed Sun.

Tel: 01776 705544   Web: www.dumgal.gov.uk

Cawdor Castle

[Map: 50; D5] On B9090, off A96, 5 miles SW of Nairn, Cawdor, Highlands.
(NGR: NH 847499 LR: 27)

One of the most impressive strongholds in Scotland, Cawdor Castle incorporates a tall and plain keep dating from the 14th century. It stands in a courtyard and the parapet and upper works were added in 1454. The castle has a deep ditch crossed by a drawbridge, and there are gabled ranges, crowned with turrets. Defending the entrance is a massive iron yett, brought here from Lochindorb Castle after 1455. There are magnificent gardens and fine grounds.

The title 'Thane of Cawdor' is associated with Macbeth, but Duncan was not murdered here – as the castle is not nearly old enough – and anyway he died following a battle near Spynie. One story is that the Calders are descended from a brother of Macbeth. The site for the castle was chosen in an unlikely manner: the location was decided by the rovings of a donkey and where it rested, by a tree, the castle was built. The remains of this tree are in the vaulted basement, and it died about 1372 when the castle was built. The tree was long believed to be a hawthorn but investigation has proved it to be a holly tree.

The 5th Thane built much of the present castle, but the Campbells obtained Cawdor in 1511 by kidnapping the girl heiress, Muriel Calder, and marrying her at the age of 12 to the Earl of Argyll's son, Sir John Campbell. Campbell of Inverliver led the kidnapping, and all six of his sons were slain. The Campbells of Cawdor, her descendants, remained at the castle, and were made Earls Cawdor in 1827. Bonnie Prince Charlie had visited in 1746.

A ghost in a blue velvet dress has reputedly been seen here, as has an apparition of John Campbell, 1st Lord Cawdor.

Fine collections of portraits, furnishings and tapestries. Explanatory displays. Gift shops. Licensed restaurant and snack bar. Gardens, grounds and nature trails. Golf course and putting. Disabled access to grounds; some of castle. Car and coach parking. Group concessions. Conferences. £££. Holiday accommodation available.

Open May-early Oct, daily 10.00-17.30; last 30 mins before closing.

Tel: 01667 404615   Web: www.cawdorcastle.com

Clackmannan Tower (HS)

[Map: 51; H5] Off B910, 7 miles E of Stirling, W outskirts of Clackmannan. (NGR: NS 905920 LR: 58)
Standing on the summit of King's Seat Hill in a commanding position, Clackmannan Tower is a large and impressive tower house. It dates from the 14th century, and was later altered to L-plan with the addition of a taller tower. There was a later mansion but this has been demolished.

It was a property of the Bruces from 1359 until 1796. The family were bankrupted by 1708, and Henry Bruce of Clackmannan fought for the Jacobites in the 1745 Rising. In the adjoining but now demolished mansion, Henry Bruce's widow 'knighted' Robert Burns with the sword of Robert the Bruce in 1787.

Access at all reasonable times: view from exterior only.

Claypotts Castle (HS)

[Map: 52; G6] Off A92, 3.5 miles E of Dundee, Angus. (NGR: NO 452319 LR: 54)
An unusual and impressive building, Claypotts Castle is a Z-plan tower house, consisting of a rectangular main block and two large round towers, each crowned with square gabled chambers, at opposite corners. There are stair turrets between the towers and main block.

Corgarff Castle

The lands passed from the Abbey of Lindores to the Strachans about 1560, and the castle was built soon afterwards. It was sold to the Grahams in 1620, one of whom was John Graham of Claverhouse, Viscount Dundee or 'Bloody Clavers'. Graham was slain in 1689 at the victory over the forces of William and Mary at Killiecrankie. His lands were forfeited by 1694 and went to the Douglas Earl of Angus, then later to the Homes. In the 19th century the castle was used to house farm labourers.

The castle is said to be haunted by a 'White Lady', reputedly the ghost of Marion Ogilvie, mistress (and wife) of Cardinal David Beaton; and Claypotts is also said to have had a brownie.

Parking Nearby. £.

Tel to check: 01786 431324

Corgarff Castle (HS)

[Map: 53; E5] Off A939, 10 miles NW of Ballater, Corgarff, Aberdeenshire.
(NGR: NJ 255086 LR: 37)
Surrounded by hills and located in a remote and picturesque spot, Corgarff Castle is an altered rectangular tower house, which dates from the 16th century. The tower rises to four storeys and the walls

Corgarff Castle

are white-washed. There are later pavilions and star-shaped outworks.

The castle was built about 1530 by the Elphinstones, and leased to the Forbes family. The castle was torched in 1571 by Adam Gordon of Auchindoun, killing Margaret Campbell, wife of Forbes of Towie, and 26 others of her household (although an alternative location for this event has been given as Towie Castle). The Erskine Earls of Mar acquired the lands in 1626, but the castle was burnt by Jacobites in 1689, then again in 1716, this time by Hanoverians to punish the Earl of Mar for his part in the Jacobite Rising, and for a third time in 1746, this time by retreating Jacobites.

Two years later the government bought Corgarff, remodelled the tower, and used it as a barracks, then to help stop illicit whisky distilling. One of the floors has a restored barrack room. Some   stories tell that the castle is haunted following the torching in 1571, and it is said that ghostly screams have been heard here.

Short but steep walk to castle. Exhibition: one of the floors houses a restored barrack room.
Explanatory displays. Gift shop. Car and coach parking. Group concessions. £.

Open Apr-Sep, daily 9.30-18.30; open Oct-Mar, wknds only 9.30-16.30; last ticket 30 mins before closing.

Tel: 01975 651460

Coulter Motte (HS)

[Map: 54; H5] On A73, 1.5 miles SW of Biggar, Coulter, Lanarkshire. (NGR: NT 018362 LR: 72)

The earthworks of an early castle, which is a fine example of a large motte and the remains of the bailey.

Parking nearby.

Access at all reasonable times.

Craigdarroch House

[Map: 55; I5] Off B729, 2 miles W of Moniaive, Craigdarroch, Dumfries and Galloway.
(NGR: NX 741909 LR: 77)

Craigdarroch House was built by William Adam in the 1720s, and is an elegant classical edifice. An L-plan tower house or dwelling is incorporated into the building, including a turnpike stair and heraldic panels. Craigdarroch was damaged by fire in 1984, but has been restored.

The lands were held by the Fergussons of Craigdarroch, who may have been descended from the 12th-century Fergus, Lord of Galloway. Alexander Fergusson had the mansion built and married Annie Laurie, the subject (or object) of the famous song. The Fergussons opposed the Jacobites, and fled from the house in 1745 when Bonnie Prince Charlie arrived here. The house was pillaged and ransacked. The Fergussons held the property until 1962 when it was sold to the Sykes family.
No WCs.

Open Jul, daily 14.00-16.00.

Tel: 01848 200202

Craigievar Castle (NTS)

[Map: 56; E6] Off A980, 4.5 miles S of Alford, Aberdeenshire. (NGR: NJ 566095 LR: 37)

A well-preserved and attractive pink-washed edifice, Craigievar Castle is a massive L-plan tower house of seven storeys. Turrets, gables, chimney-stacks and corbelling crown the upper storeys; in contrast to the lower storeys, which are very plain. It lies in a pretty spot amidst the rolling hills of Aberdeenshire.

The hall is a magnificent vaulted apartment, with mixed groin- and barrel-vaulting, and a fine plaster ceiling, and has a large fireplace with ornamental stone carving. The floors above are occupied by many chambers, reached by five turret stairs. Many of these rooms are panelled, and there is also contemporary plasterwork.

Craigmillar Castle

The property belonged to the Mortimer family from 1457, who began the castle. They ran out of money, and it was sold to the Forbeses of Menie, who completed the building in 1626. The castle passed to The National Trust for Scotland in 1963. The Blue Room is supposedly haunted by the ghost a Gordon, who was thrown from one of the windows; while another spirit is said to be that of a fiddler, drowned in a well in the kitchen, who only is witnessed by members of the Forbes family.

Guided tours only. No coaches. No groups. £££.

Open Easter-Oct, Fri-Tue 12.00-17.30, last entry 45 mins before closing; grounds all year, daily 9.30-sunset.

Tel: 01339 883635

Craigmillar Castle (HS)

[Map: 57; H5] Off A68, 3 miles SE of Edinburgh Castle, Craigmillar, Edinburgh.
(NGR: NT 288709 LR: 66)

With magnificent views over the surrounding area, Craigmillar Castle is a strong, impressive and substantial ruin. It consists of a 14th-century L-plan keep, surrounded by a curtain wall with round corner towers, which dates from the next century. Early in the 16th century the castle was given an additional walled courtyard, which is defended by a ditch.

The Prestons held the property from 1374, and built a new castle on the site of an older stronghold. In 1477 James III imprisoned his brother John, Earl of Mar, in one of its cellars, where the Earl died. James V visited the castle to escape 'the pest' in Edinburgh. The Earl of Hertford burnt the castle in 1544, after valuables placed here by the citizens of Edinburgh had been pillaged by the English.

Mary, Queen of Scots, used Craigmillar often, and fled here in 1566 after the murder of Rizzio by, among others, her second husband Darnley. It was also here that the Regent Moray, the Earl of Borthwick and Maitland of Lethington plotted Darnley's murder. Mary's son, James VI, stayed here, and the property was bought by the Gilmours in 1660. A walled-up skeleton was found in one of the vaults in 1813.

Exhibition and visitor centre. Gift shop. Refreshments. WC. Disabled WC. Car and coach parking. Group concessions. £.

Open all year: Apr-Sep, daily 9.30-18.30; Oct-Mar, Sat-Wed 9.30-16.30, closed Thu & Fri; last ticket 30 mins before closing; closed 25/26 Dec and 1/2 Jan.

Tel: 0131 661 4445

Craignethan Castle (HS)

[Map: 58; H5] Off A72, 4.5 miles W of Lanark, Craignethan, Lanarkshire. (NGR: NS 816464 LR: 72)

In a lovely position on a promontory above a deep ravine, Craignethan is an early castle built to withstand artillery. A strong tower was surrounded by a curtain wall on three sides, with a massively thick rampart protecting the landward side. There was also an outer courtyard. Much of the castle is

now ruinous, although the main tower survives more or less to the wallhead. A notable feature is the caponier in the ditch, a defensive measure, but which must have been quite claustrophobic and airless when used.

Sir James Hamilton of Finnart, a talented architect and the King's Superintendent of Palaces, built most of the castle. Hamilton was beheaded for treason in 1540, although his son eventually inherited his lands. Mary, Queen of Scots, is said to have spent the night here before the Battle of Langside in 1568. The Hamiltons formed the main part of her army, but were defeated by the Regent Moray, and Mary fled to England. The garrison of Craignethan surrendered after the battle, but the castle was retaken by the Hamiltons. It was attacked in 1579, then given up without a siege. It was slighted, and much of the defences demolished. It passed to the Hays in 1665.

The are several stories of ghosts and apparitions, including the figure of a woman wearing 'Stuart-period' dress and a headless spectre, identified by some as Mary, Queen of Scots. Manifestations have also been reported in the newer house in the courtyard.

Exhibition and explanatory boards. Gift shop. Tearoom. Car parking. Group concessions. £.

Open Apr-Sep, daily 9.30-18.30; Oct, Sat-Wed 9.30-16.30, closed Thu & Fri; Nov-Mar wknds only, 9.30-16.30; last ticket 30 mins before closing; closed 25/26 Dec and 1/2 Jan.

Tel: 01555 860364

Crathes Castle (NTS)

[Map: 59; E6] Off A93, 3 miles E of Banchory, Kincardine & Deeside. (NGR: NO 734968 LR: 45)

One of the best castles in Scotland, Crathes is a massive tower house, dating from the 16th century and square in plan. The upper storeys are adorned with much corbelling, turrets, and ornamentation, while the lower storeys are very plain, apart from a large modern window. The interior is particularly fine with original painted ceilings and a long gallery on the top floor, while the hall has

Crichton Castle

a carved fireplace which dates from the building the castle. There is a splendid walled garden with many unusual plants, and topiary and yew hedges. The grounds have waymarked trails.

The property was held by the Burnetts of Leys from the 14th century, and their original castle was in the Loch of Leys (which has been drained). The jewelled ivory 'Horn of Leys' is kept at Crathes, and was given to the Burnetts in 1323 by Robert the Bruce. Around 1553 the family began to build the new castle at Crathes, although it was not completed until 1596. The property passed to The National Trust for Scotland in 1951.

The Green Lady's Room has both an original painted ceiling and a ghost story. It is said that an apparition of a girl in a green dress has been repeatedly seen, crossing the chamber and sometimes with a baby in its arms. The tale goes that in the 19th century the skeleton of an infant was found by workmen under the hearthstone. The ghost is said to have been witnessed by Queen Victoria.

Collections of portraits and furniture. Gift shop. Restaurant. Gardens, grounds and adventure playground. Plant sales. Disabled facilities, including access to ground floor and WC. Car and coach parking. £££.
Open all year: Apr-Sep, daily 10.30-17.30, last entry 45 mins before closing; Oct, daily 10.00-16.30; Nov-Mar, Thu-Sun 10.00-15.45; grounds open all year, 9.00-sunset.
Tel: 01330 844525

Crichton Castle (HS)

[Map: 60; H6] Off B6367, 2 miles E of Gorebridge, Crichton, Midlothian.
(NGR: NT 380612 LR: 66)
In an elevated position above the Tyne, Crichton is a complex and fascinating building and is in a pleasant rural location. The ruin consists of ranges of buildings, dating from the 14th to 16th centuries, enclosing a small courtyard. One especially notable feature is the arcaded, diamond-faced facade of a 16th-century range, decorated in Italian Renaissance style. There are also the substantial ruins of the stables.

The castle was a property of the Crichtons, and probably first built about 1370. Sir William Crichton, Chancellor of Scotland, entertained the young Earl of Douglas and his brother here before having them murdered in 1440 at the 'Black Dinner' in Edinburgh Castle. John Forrester slighted the castle in retaliation.

The Crichtons were forfeited for treason in 1488, and the property later passed to Patrick Hepburn, Lord Hailes, who was made Earl of Bothwell. Mary, Queen of Scots, attended a wedding here in 1562. Crichton passed to Francis Stewart, Earl of Bothwell, who built the arcaded range, but he was also forfeited. It then passed through the hands of many families, was abandoned, and became a romantic ruin: Turner painted the castle and Sir Walter Scott used it in 'Marmion'.

It is said to be haunted by a horsemen who is reported to be seen riding up to the castle and entering it through the original entrance, which is now blocked. The bogle of Sir William Crichton reputedly haunts the stables.

Walk to property. Sales area.
Car and coach parking. Group concessions. £.
Open Apr-Sep, daily 9.30-18.30; last entry 30 mins before closing.
Tel: 01875 320017

Crookston Castle (HS)

[Map: 61; H4] Off A736, 3 miles E of Paisley, off Brockburn Road, Crookston, Glasgow.
(NGR: NS 524628 LR: 64)

Surrounded by a large ditch (now by a housing estate), Crookston Castle is an unusual ruined irregularly-shaped keep, dating from the 13th century. It was strengthened by corner towers, only one of which is fairly intact, formerly making it X-plan.

The lands passed by marriage in the 13th century to the Stewart Earls of Lennox. During the rebellion of the Earl of Lennox in the 15th century, James IV bombarded the castle with the large cannon, 'Mons Meg', now kept at Edinburgh Castle, leading to a quick surrender. Henry Stewart, Lord Darnley, owned Crookston, and he may have been betrothed to Mary, Queen of Scots, here (rather than at Wemyss Castle) or to have stayed here together after their marriage. It passed through many families, including the Graham Dukes of Montrose, who in 1757 sold it to the Maxwells of Pollok. The castle became ruinous, but was partly restored in 1847 to commemorate Queen Victoria's first visit to Glasgow. This was the first property to be held by The National Trust for Scotland, and was gifted to the trust in 1931.

Parking nearby.
Tel for details. Owned by NTS; administered by Historic Scotland.
Tel: 0141 883 9606

Cubbie Roo's Castle (HS)

[Map: 62; A6] North side of island of Wyre, Orkney. (NGR: HY 442264 LR: 6)

Standing on a small ridge, Cubbie Roo's Castle is a small keep surrounded by several rock-cut ditches, and dates from the 12th century. The keep was square in plan, and the entrance would have been at first-floor level. There are also foundations of later buildings.

The name Cubbie Roo is a corruption of Kolbein Hruga, a Norseman who built the tower about 1150, as mentioned in the Orkneyinga Saga. The assassins of Earl John Haraldsson sought refuge here in 1231, and managed to fend off attacks by the Earl's friends. Orkney did not become part of Scotland until 1468. The nearby ruinous chapel of St Mary also dates from the 12th century.

Access at all reasonable times.

Culross Palace (NTS)

[Map: 63; H5] Off B9037, 6.5 miles W of Dunfermline, Culross, Fife. (NGR: NS 986862 LR: 65)

Lying in the picturesque burgh of Culross on the north bank of the Forth, the Palace was built between 1597 and 1611, and consists of yellow-washed ranges of corbiestepped gabled buildings, with decorative paint work and fine original interiors. There is an unusual steeply terraced garden which goes up the hill at the back of the buildings.

The Palace was built by Sir George Bruce of Carnock, who made a fortune in coal mining, but about 1700 passed to the Erskines. The building has been carefully restored by The National Trust for Scotland.

The Trust has a visitor centre and exhibition in the Town House of 1626, and the house of 1610,

called The Study, is also open to visitors to view the Norwegian painted ceiling in the drawing room. Many other 16th- and 17th-century houses survive in the narrow streets of this ancient royal burgh, and can be viewed from outside.

Audio-visual show. Explanatory displays. Tea room. Town trail. Induction loop & Braille guide. ££. Combined ticket for Palace, Study and Town House available (£££).

Palace, Study and Town House, open Easter-Sep, daily 12.00-17.00, last 30 mins before closing, tearoom open 11.00-17.00, shop open 12.00-17.00.

Tel: 01383 880359

Culzean Castle (NTS)

[Map: 64; I4] Off A77, 4.5 miles W of Maybole, Culzean, Ayrshire. (NGR: NS 233103 LR: 70)

Pronounced 'Cul-lane' and set in hundreds of acres of parkland by the shore of the Firth of Clyde, Culzean Castle is a magnificent sprawling castellated mansion. It was built between 1777-92 by the architect Robert Adam, but incorporates much of the original castle, which itself was built on the site of an older stronghold. The elegant interior includes the magnificent Oval Staircase and the Circular Saloon.

Culzean was a property of the Kennedys from the 12th century. Thomas Kennedy of Culzean was murdered by the Mure Lord Auchendrane in the course of a feud. The castle was completely rebuilt for the 9th and 10th Earls of Cassillis. In 1945 it passed to The National Trust for Scotland. A flat within the building was reserved for use by President Dwight Eisenhower for his services to Britain during World War II.

The country park has many attractions, including woodland walks, a visitor centre, walled garden, adventure playground, restaurants and shops.

Fine interiors. Collections of paintings and furniture. Gift shops. Two restaurants. WC. Picnic areas. Woodland walks. Gardens and adventure playground. Country park and visitor centre – one of the foremost attractions in Scotland. Car and coach parking. Group concessions. £££.

Castle, visitor centre, restaurants and shops open Apr-Oct, daily 10.30-17.30, last entry 90 mins before closing; shop, open Nov-22 Dec, Sat-Sun 10.00-16.00; visitor facilities (not castle) also open 20 Jan-24 Mar, Sat-Sun 10.00-16.00; country park open all year, daily 9.30-sunset.

Tel: 01655 884455

Dalmeny House

[Map: 65; H5] Off A90, 6 miles NW of Edinburgh, South Queensferry. (NGR: NT 167779 LR: 65)

Home to the Earl and Countess of Rosebery, whose family have lived here for over 300 years, Dalmeny House dates from 1815 and was built in Tudor Gothic style. There are vaulted corridors and a splendid hammerbeam hall, but the main rooms are in classical style. It replaced an earlier house. The house has French furniture, tapestries and porcelain, as well as 18th-century portraits by Gainsborough, Raeburn, Reynolds and Lawrence, racing mementoes, and items associated with Napoleon. There are fine walks in the wooded grounds and along the shore.

The lands were held by the Mowbrays, but were sold to the Hamilton Earl of Haddington in 1615 and then to the Primroses in 1662, who were made Earls of Rosebery in 1703. Archibald Primrose, 5th Earl, was Foreign Secretary in 1886 and 1892-4, then Prime Minister from 1894-5.

Guided tours. Tea room. Disabled access and WC. Car and coach parking. Group concessions. ££.

Open Jul-Aug, Sun-Tue 14.00-17.30; last entry 60 mins before closing; open other times by appt only.

Tel: 0131 331 1888   Web: www.dalmeny.co.uk

Dean Castle

[Map: 66; H4] Off B7038, 1 mile NE of Kilmarnock, Ayrshire. (NGR: NS 437394 LR: 70)

Standing in a country park, Dean Castle consists of a 14th-century keep of three storeys and a 15th-century palace block within a courtyard, all enclosed by a curtain wall.

The lands were given to the Boyds by Robert the Bruce, and a castle here is said to have been besieged by the English. Robert Boyd became Guardian of James III, and practically ruled Scotland from 1466-9. He later had to flee to Denmark, and his brother was executed for treason. William, 10th Lord Boyd, was created Earl of Kilmarnock in 1661. William, 4th Earl, was Privy Councillor to Bonnie Prince Charlie during the Jacobite Rising of 1745. He was a Colonel in the Prince's guard, but was captured after Culloden in 1746 and executed by beheading. His property and titles were forfeited, although the family recovered the estates just two years later. The execution, however, was apparently foretold when before the Rising servants were terrified by an apparition of Boyd's severed head rolling about the floor in the castle.

Dean was restored from 1905 after part fell ruinous, and now houses a museum with displays including a copy of the 'Kilmarnock Edition' of Robert Burns's work.

Guided tours. Explanatory displays. Museum of armour and musical instruments. Gift shop. Restaurant. WC. Picnic area. Park. Disabled access – but not into castle. Car and coach parking. Country park and castle free.

Open daily Apr-Oct 12.00-17.00; open Nov to end Mar wknds only; closed Christmas and New Year; park open daily dawn-dusk. (Castle closed for renovation until mid June 2005).
Tel: 01563 522702   Web: www.deancastle.com

Delgatie Castle

[Map: 67; D6] Off A947, 2 miles E of Turriff, Banff and Buchan, Aberdeenshire.
(NGR: NJ 755506 LR: 29)

A tall and imposing castle, Delgatie consists of a 15th-century keep, although the building may incorporate work of some 400 years earlier. There is an adjoining gabled house, and lower later buildings, and the castle has fine interiors, including painted ceilings from the 1590s. The hall has a vaulted ceiling and the fireplace dates from the 16th century.

Delgatie was held by the Comyn Earls of Buchan, but passed to the Hays in the 14th century, and they were made Earls of Errol in 1452. Sir Gilbert Hay of Delgatie, with many others of the family, were killed at Flodden in 1513. Mary, Queen of Scots, spent three days here in 1562. Francis, 9th Earl, was summoned for treason in 1594 for supporting the Gordon Earl of Huntly, and part of the west wall was battered down by James VI's forces.

Sir William Hay of Delgatie was standard bearer to the Marquis of Montrose. Although defeated at Philiphaugh in 1645, Hay managed to return the standard to Buchanan Castle. He was executed

with Montrose at Edinburgh five years later, and buried beside him in St Giles Cathedral.

Delgatie had to be sold in 1762, but was bought back by the Hays who began the task of restoration, and the castle was made the Clan Hay centre in 1948. It is said to be haunted by the ghost known as Rohaise, a feisty young woman who is believed to have defended the castle from an attack. She is said to haunt the bedroom off the main stair, which now bears her name; and to visit men who stay in the chamber.

Many rooms, two with original painted ceilings of 1592 and 1597. Guided tours available by arrangement. Explanatory boards. Collection of portraits. Gift shop. Tearoom. WC. Picnic area. Disabled access to tearoom and front hall only. Accommodation available including in castle. Short breaks available. £

Open Apr-Oct, daily 10.00-17.00.

Tel: 01888 563479   Web: www.delgatiecastle.com

Dirleton Castle (HS)

[Map: 68; H6] Off A198, 2 miles W of North Berwick, Dirleton, East Lothian. (NGR: NT 518840 LR: 66)

Standing on a rock in the pretty village of the same name, Dirleton is an outstanding ruinous castle with a complex of towers and ranges around a courtyard, which were once surrounded by a wide ditch. The old part of the castle, dating from the 13th century, is grouped around a small triangular court, and consists of a large drum tower, a smaller round tower and a rectangular tower. It was extended and rebuilt down the years, the main entrance is over a deep ditch, and there is a large doocot.

The castle was built by the Vaux family. It was captured after a hard-fought battle in 1298, when the English employed large siege engines, but was retaken by the Scots in 1311 and partly demolished. In the 15th century the castle passed to the Halyburton family, who extended it; and in the 16th century to the Ruthvens, who again did much remodelling; then in 1600 to the Erskines of Gogar.

In 1650 the castle was besieged during Cromwell's invasion of Scotland, and quickly forced to surrender: three of the leaders of the garrison were subsequently shot. The castle was abandoned soon afterwards, and became ruinous. There are fine gardens with ancient yews and hedges around the bowling green, as well as a fine early 20th-century Arts and Crafts garden and recreated Victorian garden.

Explanatory displays. Gift shop. WC. Limited disabled access. Disabled WC. Car and coach parking. Group concessions. £

Open all year: Apr-Sep, daily 9.30-18.30; Oct-Mar, daily 9.30-16.30; last ticket sold 30 mins before closing; closed 25/26 Dec and 1/2 Jan. Owned by NTS; administered by Historic Scotland.

Tel: 01620 850330

Doune Castle

Doune Castle (HS)

[Map: 69; G5] Off A820, 7 miles NW of Stirling, SE of Doune, Stirlingshire. (NGR: NN 728011 LR: 57)

Standing on a strong site in a lovely location above the River Teith, Doune Castle dates from the 14th century and has two strong towers linked by a lower range. These buildings form two sides of a courtyard, the other sides enclosed by a high curtain wall. The fine Lord's Hall has a carved oak screen, musician's gallery and an impressive double fireplace. There are good views from the top of the tower.

The castle was built by Robert Stewart, Duke of Albany, who virtually ruled Scotland during the reign of Robert III and the imprisonment in England of the young James I. When Albany died in 1420, his son, Murdoch, succeeded him as Regent, but when James I was freed in 1424 he had Murdoch executed.

Doune was kept as a royal hunting lodge, prison, and dower house for the widows of James III, James IV and James V. It was occasionally used by Mary, Queen of Scots, and was held by forces loyal to her until 1570. This is another castle where a ghostly apparition of Mary has been reported. Doune was occupied by the Marquis of Montrose in 1645, and by Government troops during the Jacobite risings of 1689 and 1715. It was taken by Jacobites in 1745, and used as a prison, although many of the prisoners escaped. Doune was restored in the late 19th century, and was used as a location for the film 'Monty Python and the Holy Grail'.

Explanatory displays. Gift shop. Picnic area. Car parking. Group concessions. £.

Open all year: Apr-Sep, daily 9.30-18.30; Oct-Mar, Sat-Wed 9.30-16.30, closed Thu & Fri; last admission 30 mins before closing; closed 25/26 Dec and 1/2 Jan.

Tel: 01786 841742

Druchtag Motte (HS)

[Map: 70; J4] Off A747, 11 miles NW of Whithorn, Mochrum, Dumfries and Galloway.
 (NGR: NX 349467 LR: 82)

Druchtag is the well-preserved motte of a 12th or 13th century. The lands of Druchtag are mentioned in 1577 and later, and were part of the Monreith estate, which was held by the MacCullochs, and then the Maxwells.

Access at all reasonable times – steep climb to top.

Drum Castle (NTS)

[Map: 71; E6] Off A93, 9.5 miles W of Aberdeen, 3 miles W of Peterculter, Kincardine and Deeside. (NGR: NJ 796005 LR: 38)

One of the oldest occupied houses in Scotland and surrounded by extensive grounds, Drum Castle consists of a plain 13th-century keep of four storeys. To this was added a large L-shaped range of 1619, and the castle was extended again in the 19th century.

Drum Castle

There is a small courtyard completed by a wall and gateway, as well as a walled garden with old roses and the Old Wood of Drum, an ancient oak woodland.

Drum was a property of the Irvines from 1323, when the lands were given to them by Robert the Bruce after Sir William de Irwyn, or Irvine, whose seat was at Bonshaw, had been his standard bearer. Sir Alexander Irvine was killed at the Battle of Harlaw in 1411, slain by and slaying MacLean of Duart 'Hector of the Battles'. The Irvines supported Charles I, and Drum was besieged and plundered by Argyll in 1644, and sacked again in 1645 when the womenfolk were turned out of the castle. The family were Jacobites and fought in the 1715 and 1745 Jacobite Risings. Alexander, 17th of Drum, fought at Culloden, although he managed to escape both the aftermath of the battle and forfeiture, after hiding in a secret chamber at Drum. In 1975 the castle was given to The National Trust for Scotland.

Collections of furniture and pictures. Garden of historic roses. Woodland walks. Gift shop. Tearoom. WC. Disabled facilities. Parking. £££.

Castle and garden open Easter or Apr-Sep: Apr, May, Jun & Sep, daily 12.30-17.30; Jul-Aug, daily 10.00-17.30, last entry 45 mins before closing; also some wknds in winter; grounds all year, daily 9.30-sunset.

Tel: 01330 811204

Drumcoltran Tower (HS)

[Map: 72; J5] Off A711, 6 miles NE of Dalbeattie, Drumcoltran, Dumfries and Galloway.
(NGR: NX 869683 LR: 84)

Located in the midst of farm buildings, Drumcoltran Tower is a 16th-century L-plan tower house. It rises to three storeys and an attic and, although roofed, does not have internal flooring. It was built by the Maxwells, but sold to the Irvines in 1669, then the Hynds, the Herons, and then the Maxwells again in 1875. The tower was occupied until the 1890s.

Parking.

Access at all reasonable times.

Drumlanrig Castle

[Map: 73; I5] Off A76, 3 miles NW of Thornhill, Drumlanrig, Dumfries and Galloway.
(NGR: NX 851992 LR: 78)

Set in fine parkland and grounds, Drumlanrig is an impressive 17th-century mansion. It consists of ranges enclosing a courtyard and higher rectangular towers at the corners, which have pepper-pot turrets. Work from a 14th-century castle, including cellars, are built into the mansion.

The original castle was built by the Douglases soon after 1357, but was sacked by the English in 1549. It was destroyed in 1575 because the family supported Mary, Queen of Scots, who had stayed here in 1563. The building was rebuilt and James VI stayed here in 1617, and then Drumlanrig was occupied by a Cromwellian force in 1650. A huge new mansion was built between 1675 and 1689 by the architect William Wallace for William Douglas, 3rd Earl of Queensberry, who was made Duke in 1684. Bonnie Prince Charlie had stayed at the castle in 1746 after retreat from Derby, and his men sacked the building, stabbing a painting of William of Orange. Drumlanrig passed to the Scott Dukes of Buccleuch in 1810. The castle was restored later in that century, and there is a fine collection of pictures, including paintings by Rembrandt and Holbein, although there was a notorious theft of a Leonardo da Vinci from the castle in 2003.

Three ghosts are said to haunt the castle. One is reputed to be the spirit of Lady Anne Douglas, seen with her head under her arm; another that of a young woman in a flowing dress; and the third of a monkey or beast, witnessed in the Yellow Monkey Room.

Fine collection of pictures, including paintings by Rembrandt and Holbein, as well as many other works of art. Guided tours. Gift shop. Tea room. Visitor centre. Park land, woodland walks and gardens. Visitor centre. WC. Picnic area. Adventure woodland play area. Working craft centre. Demonstrations of birds of prey (except Thu). Disabled access. Car and coach parking. Group concessions. £££ (local residents free).

Open May-late Aug, 12.00 to daily last tour at 16.00; closed Fri in May and Jun; country park open Easter-Sep.

Tel: 01848 330248   Web: www.drumlanrig.org.uk

Drumlanrig's Tower, Hawick

[Map: 74; I6] Off A7, Hawick, Borders. (NGR: NT 502144 LR: 79)

In the Border town of Hawick, Drumlanrig's Tower is an altered and extended L-plan tower house, dating from the 16th century and formerly surrounded by a moat. It was a property of the Douglases of Drumlanrig, and the only building left unburnt after the torching of Hawick by the English in 1570. It was later occupied by Anna, Duchess of Buccleuch, wife of the executed Duke of Monmouth. From the 17th century, part of the basement was used as a prison, this becoming the wine-cellar on its conversion to a coaching inn. The hotel was closed in 1970, and the tower was restored to house an exhibition, with 10 galleries covering 800 years of Border history.

Visitor centre. Period rooms and costumed figures. Explanatory displays. Gift shop. Disabled access. Parking nearby at Common Haugh. £.

Open early Mar-Oct, Sun 12.00-17.00; late Mar-May and Oct, Mon-Sat 10.00-17.00; Jun-Sep, Mon-Sat 10.00-17.30; Jul-Aug 10.00-18.00.

Tel: 01450 373457   Web: www.scotborders.gov.uk/outabout/museums

Drummond Castle Gardens

[Map: 75; G5] Off A822, 2.5 miles SW of Crieff, Drummond, Perthshire. (NGR: NN 844181 LR: 58)

Built on a rocky outcrop, Drummond Castle consists of a 15th-century keep to which has been added a lower 17th-century extension, and a late 19th-century mansion, which was remodelled from the buildings surrounding the keep. The castle has a splendid formal garden with terraces overlooking a magnificent parterre, celebrating the saltire and family heraldry, surrounding a famous sundial by John Milne, Master Mason to Charles I.

  Sir Malcolm Drummond distinguished himself at the Battle of Bannockburn in 1314, and was given the lands here. Margaret Drummond, daughter of the then laird, was mistress to, and possibly wife of, James IV. Some of the nobles wanted James to marry Margaret Tudor, sister of Henry VIII of England; and Margaret, and two of her sisters, were cruelly poisoned. They are buried in Dunblane Cathedral. Mary, Queen of Scots, visited the castle in 1566-7 with Bothwell, and the Drummonds were made Earls of Perth in 1605. The castle was badly damaged by Cromwell in the 1650s, and slighted after having been occupied by Hanoverian troops during the Jacobite Rising of 1715. James, 5th Earl, had commanded the Jacobite cavalry at the Battle of Sheriffmuir that year, and the 6th, another James, commanded the left wing of the Jacobite army at Culloden in 1746. The family was forfeited, although the Earldom of Perth was recovered by them in 1853, as was Stobhall, where they now live. Drummond passed to the Willoughbys.

Gift shop. Disabled partial access. WC. Car and coach parking.

Castle not open. Gardens open Easter & May-Oct 13.00-18.00; last entry 60 mins before closing.

Tel: 01764 681433   Web: www.drummondcastlegardens.co.uk

Dryhope Tower

[Map: 76; I5] Off A708, 9 miles S of Peebles, 2 miles E of Cappercleuch, Borders. (NGR: NT 267247 LR: 73)

In a tranquil spot in the rolling hills of the Borders overlooking St Mary's Loch, Dryhope Tower is a ruinous tower house, formerly of three or four storeys and dating from the 16th century. The walls are pierced by gunloops.

Dryhope was a property of the Scotts, and was the home of Mary (or Marion) Scott, the beautiful Flower of Yarrow. The ballad the 'Dowie Dens of Yarrow' records the bloody events surrounding her, when her suitor was waylaid and slain with much bloodshed by her brothers. In 1576 she married Walter Scott of Harden, 'Auld Wat', a famous Border reiver. The tower was slighted in 1592 after the Scotts had been involved in a plot against James VI at Falkland Palace, but was rebuilt by 1613. The tower has recently been consolidated and cleared of vegetation.

Access at all reasonable times.

Duart Castle

[Map: 77; G3] Off A849, 2 miles S of Craignure, Duart, Mull. (NGR: NM 749354 LR: 49)

An impressive and daunting fortress in a prominent position on Duart Point, the castle consists of a large 12th-century curtain wall, enclosing a courtyard on a rocky knoll. In 1390 Lachlan Lubanach, 5th Chief, built the keep on the outside of the curtain wall, enclosing the existing well. There are later ranges of buildings within the walls, and the entrance was through a gatehouse with a portcullis.

The MacLeans of Duart claim descent from Gillean of the Battle Axe. Lachlan Lubanach married Lady Elizabeth, daughter of the Lord of the Isles, grand-daughter of Robert II King of Scots, and was granted the first known charter for Duart dated 1390 as her dowry. While fighting with the MacDonalds, the 6th chief Red Hector was killed at the Battle of Harlaw in 1411, slaying and being slain by Sir Alexander Irvine of Drum.

Lachlan Cattanach, 11th Chief, became so unhappy with his Campbell wife that he had the poor woman chained to a rock in the Firth of Lorn to be drowned at high tide. However, she was rescued and taken to her father, the Campbell Earl of Argyll. As a result, MacLean was murdered in his bed in Edinburgh by Sir John Campbell of Cawdor.

In 1674 the castle and lands were acquired by the Campbell Earl of Argyll. The MacLeans remained staunch supporters of the Stewarts throughout the Jacobite Risings. Although garrisoned from time to time, the castle was not used as a residence, and was abandoned after being garrisoned during the Jacobite Rising of 1745 to become derelict and roofless. It was acquired in 1911 by Fitzroy MacLean, 26th Chief, who restored the castle.

13th-century keep, exhibitions, dungeons and state rooms. Tea room and gift shop. WC. Picnic areas. Disabled access to tea room and gift shop. Car and coach parking. ££..

Open April Sun-Thu 11.00-16.00, May-mid Oct, daily 10.30-17.30.

Tel: 01680 812309/01577 830311   Web: www.duartcastle.com

Duff House, Banff (HS)

[Map: 78; D6] Off A97, in Banff, Aberdeenshire (NGR: NJ 692633 LR: 29)
A tall and impressive building, Duff House is a fine classical mansion with colonnades and corner towers. It dates from 1735, and was built by William Adam for William Duff of Braco, later Earl of Fife, who was a very rich fellow. Despite this, Adam and Duff fell out over the expense of building

the house, and work stopped in 1741 and it was never completed as intended. The subsequent legal action was eventually won by Adam although it cost both men more than money. This is one of many castles and houses which are said to be haunted by a 'Green Lady'.
  The house is now used to display works of art from the National Galleries of Scotland. There is a programme of changing exhibitions, as well as musical and other events.
Exhibitions. Sales area. Refreshments. WC. Picnic area. Disabled facilities including lift and toilets. Parking. £ (free admission to shop, tearoom, grounds and woodland walks).
Open all summer: tel to check times etc.
Tel: 01261 818181

Duffus Castle (HS)

[Map: 79; D5] Off B9012 or B9135, 3 miles NW of Elgin, Moray. (NGR: NJ 189672 LR: 28)
A fine example of a motte and bailey castle, Duffus Castle dates from the 12th century, and has an extensive outer bailey with a wet moat, a walled and ditched inner bailey, and a large motte. On the motte was built a square 14th-century stone keep, but this was too heavy for its foundations and part has collapsed down the slope.
  The original castle was built by Freskin, Lord of Strathbrock, ancestor of both the Murrays and the Sutherlands. David I stayed here while supervising the construction of nearby Kinloss Abbey. The castle was destroyed by the Scots in 1297, but was rebuilt in stone by the Cheynes in the 14th century. It passed by marriage to the Sutherland Lord Duffus in 1350, and the family held the property until 1843. The castle was sacked in 1452 by the Douglas Earl of Moray, and again in 1645 by Royalists. John Graham of Claverhouse, 'Bonnie' Dundee' stayed here in 1689. The castle was abandoned for nearby Duffus House at the end of the 17th century.
Car parking.
Access at all reasonable times – short walk.
Tel: 01667 460232

Duffus Castle – see previous page.

Dumbarton Castle (HS)

[Map: 80; H4] Off A814, in Dumbarton. (NGR: NS 400745 LR: 64)

On a commanding rock on the north shore of the Clyde, little remains of the medieval Dumbarton Castle. Most of what remains dates from the 18th and 19th century, except the 14th-century entrance.

Meaning 'fortress of the Britons', Dumbarton is first mentioned around 450 as the stronghold of the kings of Strathclyde. In 756 it was captured by Picts and Northumbrians, and in 870 was besieged by Irish raiders, who starved the garrison into surrender. Owen the Bald, last King of Strathclyde, died at Carham in 1018, and Strathclyde was absorbed into the kingdom of Scots.

Dumbarton became a royal castle, and was a formidable fortress. William Wallace was held here before being taken to London for execution in 1305. In 1333 the young David II sheltered in the castle during fighting with the English. James IV besieged Dumbarton twice in 1489 to oust the Earl of Lennox, the second time successfully, and then used it as a base to destroy the Lord of the Isles. After the disastrous Battle of Pinkie in 1547, the infant Mary, Queen of Scots, was kept in safety from the English at Dumbarton for some months before being taken to France. The Earl of Morton and Patrick Stewart, 3rd Earl of Orkney, were imprisoned here before execution in 1581 and 1614 respectively. In 1654 a Royalist force made a successful surprise attack on Cromwell's garrison.

The castle was badly damaged during this period, and was then developed for artillery over the following centuries.

Exhibition in Governor's House. Gift shop. Refreshments. WC. Car parking. Group concessions. £.

Open all year: Apr-Sep, daily 9.30-18.30; Oct-Mar, Sat-Wed 9.30-16.30, closed Thu & Fri; last entry 30 mins before closing; closed 25/26 Dec and 1/2 Jan.

Tel: 01389 732167

Dunbar Castle

[Map: 81; H6] Off A1087, Dunbar, on N shore just W of harbour, East Lothian.
(NGR: NT 678794 LR: 67)

Although once one of the most important castles in Scotland, Dunbar Castle is now very fragmentary. The ruins date in part from the 12th century, and are in a fine location by the harbour. The castle was held by the Cospatrick Earls of Dunbar, but it was captured by the English in 1297. Black Agnes, Countess of Douglas, defended it successfully for six weeks in 1338 against English armies,

Dundonald Castle

using a giant catapult against the besiegers' stone-hurling mangonels. The 11th Earl of Dunbar was forfeited for treason; and the castle was slighted in 1488, but later rebuilt by James IV, and it was remodelled for artillery about 1515. It was burned by the English in 1548. Further fortifications were added by the French two years later, but destroyed under the terms of the Treaty of Leith. Mary, Queen of Scots, visited at least twice, once after the murder of Rizzio; and then after the murder of Darnley, after being kidnapped by the Earl of Bothwell, whom she later married. The castle surrendered and was destroyed after Mary had fled to England. Much of the ruins were demolished in the 19th century to build the harbour.

Parking nearby.

Access at all reasonable times – care should be taken as parts are dangerously ruined.

Dundonald Castle

[Map: 82; H4] Off B730, 3.5 miles SE of Irvine, Dundonald, Ayrshire. (NGR: NS 364345 LR: 70)

In a prominent location, Dundonald Castle consists of a remodelled 13th-century keep, formerly the gatehouse of an earlier castle, and said to have been slighted in the Wars of Independence. The entrance was blocked and the basement and hall on the first floor were given vaults, the hall vault being particularly fine. Most of the wall of the adjoining courtyard survives.

  Dundonald was built by the Stewarts in the 13th century, and was extended and remodelled around 1350 by Robert II, who died at Dundonald in 1390. Robert III also used the castle, and he may have died here in 1406. The property was bought by Sir William Cochrane in 1636, and he used materials from the old castle to build the mansion of Auchans – itself now a ruin. The visitor centre features an interpretive display charting the history of the castle.

Visitor centre. Gift shop. Coffee shop. WC. Disabled access only to visitor centre. Parking. £.

Open Apr-Oct, daily 10.00-17.00, last entry 30 mins before closing. Managed by the Friends of Dundonald Castle.

Tel: 01563 851489   Web: www.royaldundonaldcastle.co.uk

Dunfermline Palace (HS)

[Map: 83; H5] Off A994, Monastery Street, Dunfermline, Fife. (NGR: NT 089872 LR: 65)

In the attractive burgh of the same name, Dunfermline Palace was remodelled into a magnificent residence from the guest range of the abbey. The ruins are particularly impressive from Pittencrieff Glen, and consist of a range with wide mullioned windows and formerly elaborate vaulting.

  Dunfermline Abbey was founded about 1070 by Queen Margaret, wife of Malcolm Canmore, and

they were buried here (until the Reformation). Many other Scottish monarchs were also interred here, including Donald Bane, Edgar, Alexander I, David I, Malcolm IV, William the Lyon, Alexander III, and Robert the Bruce (except his heart). There appears to have been a royal palace from the 14th century, as Edward I stayed here in 1303-4, although he described Dunfermline as 'not a church but a den of thieves' and had the place sacked and torched. David II was born at the palace in 1323, but it may have been burned, this time by Richard II, in 1385. It was restored, and James I was born here in 1394. James IV, James V, and Mary, Queen of Scots, all visited. The palace was remodelled in 1587 by Queen Anne, wife of James VI, and Charles I was born here in 1600. Charles II used the palace in 1650, but it was abandoned soon afterwards, and unroofed by 1708.

Explanatory displays. Gift shop. Parking nearby. Group concessions. £.

Open Apr-Sep, daily 9.30-18.30; Oct-Mar, Mon-Wed and Sat 9.30-16.30, Thu 9.30-12.30, Sun 14.00-16.30, closed Fri; last ticket 30 mins before closing; choir of abbey church open Mon-Sat 10.00-16.30, Sun 14.00-16.30.

Tel: 01383 739026

Dunnideer Castle

[Map: 84; D6] Off B992, 1 mile W of Insch, 0.5 miles S of Dunnideer, in ramparts of fort and settlement, at Dunnideer. (NGR: NJ 613282 LR: 37)

Standing within the earthworks of an Iron Age fort, Dunnideer Castle is a very ruinous 13th-century castle. Parts of the walls of the fort are vitrified, indicating the ramparts had been burnt at some time. There is a sign-posted footpath and steep ascent, but there are superb views.

The stronghold is said to have been built by Gregory the Great (or Giric) around 890, and he is said to have held court with King Arthur. The present castle was probably built about 1260 by John Balliol, father of John I, Toom Tabard, who was forced to abdicate by Edward I of England in 1297. The Tyrie family occupied the castle until 1724.

Access at all reasonable times: sign-posted footpath and steep ascent.

Dunnottar Castle

[Map: 85; F7] Off A92, 2 miles S of Stonehaven, Kincardine & Deeside. (NGR: NO 882839 LR: 45)

Set on a virtually impregnable cliff-top promontory some 160 feet above the sea, Dunnottar Castle is a spectacular ruined courtyard castle, parts of which date from the 12th century. The castle consists of a 15th-century L-plan keep, 16th- and 17th-century ranges around a large courtyard, as well as a substantial chapel, stable block, forge, barracks, and priest's house.

There was a stronghold here from early times, and it was besieged by the Picts, and then in 900 by Norsemen when Donald, King of Scots, was slain. Dunnottar was captured by William Wallace from the English in 1296, one story telling that he burnt 4000 Englishmen, no doubt a slight exaggeration. Edward III of England took the castle in the 1330s and strengthened it, but it was quickly recaptured by the Scots.

The Keith Earls Marischal acquired the property in 1382, and by the beginning of the 16th century Dunnottar was one of the strongest fortresses in Scotland. Mary, Queen of Scots, stayed here in 1562. The Marquis of Montrose unsuccessfully besieged it in 1645. Six years later the Scottish crown jewels were brought here for safety, and Cromwell had the castle besieged in 1652. Before the garrison surrendered, after an eight month siege, the regalia and state papers were smuggled out to be hidden in nearby Kinneff Church until recovered at the Restoration in 1660.

In 1685 Covenanters, numbering some 167 women and men, were packed into one of the cellars during a hot summer and nine died while 25 escaped. The others, when freed, were found to have been tortured. The castle was held for William and Mary in 1689, and many Jacobites were imprisoned here. The Earl supported the Jacobites in the Rising of 1715, and was subsequently forfeited. The castle was partly dismantled by the Duke of Argyll in 1716, and again in 1718. External shots of

Dunrobin Castle

the castle were used in the film 'Hamlet' with Mel Gibson. The castle is said to be haunted by several ghosts, including the apparition of a young girl, a deer hound, a Norse-looking man, and the sounds of a meeting being conducted in Benholm's Lodging when nobody is present.

Getting to the castle involves a walk, steep climb, and a steeper one back. Exhibition. Sales area. WC. Car and coach parking. Group concessions. £.

Open Easter-Oct, Mon-Sat 9.00-18.00, Sun 14.00-17.00; winter Mon-Fri only, 9.00 to sunset; last admission 60 mins before closing.

Tel: 01569 762173   Web: www.dunechtestates.co.uk

Dunrobin Castle

[Map: 86; C5] Off A9, 1.5 miles NE of Golspie, Dunrobin, Sutherland, Highland. (NGR: NC 852008 LR: 17)

With fine gardens and in a pleasant spot, Dunrobin is an elegant fairy-tale castle, which incorporates an altered keep, which may date from the 1300s. The castle was remodelled and extended around 1780, then again in the 19th and 20th centuries.

The Sutherland family were made Earls of Sutherland in 1235, and had a castle here from the 13th century: Dunrobin may be called after Robert or Robin, the 6th Earl. At Helmsdale Castle, Isobel Sinclair poisoned John, the 11th Earl, and his wife hoping to secure the succession of her son, but the future 12th Earl escaped, and in a mix up she managed to kill her own son. Isobel poisoned herself the night before she was to be executed. The property went through an heiress to the Marquess of Stafford, and they were made Dukes of Sutherland in 1833. The family are remembered for their part in the Highland Clearances.

The upper floors of the castle are reputedly haunted by the ghost of a girl, either a daughter of the 14th Earl or a pretty young lass from an enemy clan. The story goes that she was killed by falling from the window of one of the towers, and that one of the rooms she haunted was disused, although there is said to have been no recent manifestations.

Collections of furniture, paintings and memorabilia. Museum, which features a collection of Pictish stones. Formal gardens. Guided tours. Explanatory displays. Gift shop. Tea room. WC. Disabled access: phone to arrange. Car and coach parking. Group concessions. £££.

Open Apr-mid Oct: Apr, May and Oct, Mon-Sat 10.30-16.00, Sun 12.00-16.00; Jun and Sep, Mon-Sat 10.30-17.30, Sun 12.00-17.30; Jul and Aug, daily 10.30-17.30; last entry 30 mins before closing.

Tel: 01408 633177   Web: www.highlandescape.com

Dunstaffnage Castle (HS)

[Map: 87; G3] Off A85, 3.5 miles NE of Oban, Dunstaffnage, Argyll. (NGR: NM 882344 LR: 49)

In a fine wooded spot on a promontory in the Firth of Lorn, Dunstaffnage Castle is an impressive ruin. There is a tall and massive 13th-century curtain wall with round towers, and a 16th-century gatehouse, which was later much altered and is still roofed. Ruinous ranges of buildings housed a hall and kitchen.

A stronghold here was held by the kings of Dalriada in the 7th century, and was one of the places that the Stone of Destiny was kept. The present castle was built by the MacDougalls, but was be-

sieged and captured by Robert the Bruce in 1309, and Bruce made the castle a royal property with the Campbells as keepers. James IV visited twice. The 9th Earl of Argyll burned the castle in 1685 during his rebellion of the same year. In 1715 and 1746 government troops occupied the castle during the Jacobite Risings, and Flora MacDonald was briefly imprisoned here after helping Bonnie Prince Charlie. There is a fine ruinous chapel nearby in an atmospheric setting.

The castle is said to be haunted by a ghost in a green dress, the 'Ell-maid of Dunstaffnage' and her appearance heralds events, both bad and good, in the lives of the Campbells. Ghostly footsteps, as heavy as a booted man, have also been reported in the gatehouse, as well as bangs and thumps.

Explanatory panels. Gift shop. WC. Car and coach parking. Group concessions. £.

Open Apr-Sep, daily 9.30-18.30; Oct-Mar, Sat-Wed 9.30-16.30, closed Thu & Fri; last ticket 30 mins before closing; closed 25/26 Dec and 1/2 Jan.

Tel: 01631 562465

Duntulm Castle

Duntulm Castle

[Map: 88; D2] Off A855, 6.5 miles N of Uig, Duntulm, Skye. (NGR: NG 410743 LR: 23)

On a beautiful but strong site protected by cliffs and steep slopes, Duntulm Castle stands above the sea with wonderful views across to the outer isles on a clear day. Although it was once a secure and comfortable fortress and residence, the remaining buildings are very ruinous.

Duntulm was originally an Iron Age fortress later used by Norsemen, and then known as Dundavid or Dun Dhaibhidh. It was held by the MacLeods and then the MacDonalds of Sleat in the 16th century. James V visited the castle in 1540. Around 1700 Hugh MacDonald was starved to death in a dungeon after being given only salted beef and no water, and died raving: his ghostly groans are said to then have been heard. The castle was abandoned around 1730 when the MacDonalds moved to Monkstadt House, then Armadale Castle in Sleat. The castle has many other ghost stories, and the bogles are said to be one reason why the MacDonalds moved to Monkstadt: another might be the exposed, narrow and windswept position of Duntulm.

Parking Nearby.

View from exterior – care must be taken as dangerously ruined.

Dunure Castle

[Map: 89; I4] Off A719, 5 miles NW of Maybole, Ayrshire. (NGR: NS 253158 LR: 70)

Once a strong fortress on the summit of a rock by the sea, Dunure Castle consists of a ruined 13th-century keep, surrounded by a curtain wall, and a 15th-century block, at lower level, containing kitchens, a hall and private chambers.

Dunure was a property of the Kennedys. One of the family married Mary, daughter of Robert III, and another was Bishop of St Andrews and founded St Salvator's College. In 1570 Allan Stewart, Commendator of Crossraguel Abbey, was roasted in sop here by the Kennedy Earl of Cassillis until he signed away the lands of the abbey. Kennedy of Bargany, an enemy of Cassillis, hearing of the treatment of Stewart, stormed the castle and rescued the Commendator. Cassillis was instructed to pay Stewart a pension, although he kept the lands, and led to a feud with the Kennedys of Bargany. By 1696 the castle was abandoned and ruined.

Ghostly cries have reputedly been heard emanating from the chamber in which Stewart was roasted. *Parking Nearby.*

Access at all reasonable times.

Dunvegan Castle

[Map: 90; D2] Off A850, 1 mile N of Dunvegan, Skye. (NGR: NG 247491 LR: 23)

On what was once an island in Loch Dunvegan to the north of Skye is Dunvegan Castle. The castle has been continuously occupied by the chiefs of MacLeod since 1270, who trace their ancestry back to Leod, a son of Olaf the Black, Norse King of the Isle of Man. His stronghold was developed down the centuries into a large mansion and castle, and it is still owned by the 29th Chief of MacLeod. The MacLeods supported Robert the Bruce in the Wars of Independence, and they fought at the bloody battle of Harlaw in 1411. Dunvegan was visited by James V in 1540, and the king was reputedly entertained on the top of MacLeod's Tables, flat-topped hills. The MacLeods fought at the Battle of Worcester for Charles II but lost 500 men, which made them reluctant to take part in the Jacobite Rising.

The castle is the home to the famous Fairy Flag, now reduced in size and somewhat threadbare. One story is that it was given to one of the chiefs by his fairy wife at their parting, and it is credited with many supernatural powers. The flag, however, originates from the Middle East, and it has been dated between 400 and 700 AD. Other items at Dunvegan include a drinking horn, 'Rory Mor's Horn', holding several pints of claret, which the heir of the MacLeods had to empty in one go; and the Dunvegan Cup, gifted to the clan by the O'Neils of Ulster in 1596. There are also mementoes of

Bonnie Prince Charlie and Flora MacDonald, and information about St Kilda, which was formerly a property of the family.

Info cards in various languages in each of the public rooms. Guides on-hand. Audio-visual theatre. Gift shops. Restaurant. WC. Gardens. Boat trips (££) to seal colony. Dunvegan seal colony. Pedigree Highland cattle fold. Car and coach parking. Group/student/OAP concessions. Holiday cottages available, also wedding venue. £££.

Open all year: Mar-Oct, daily 10.00-17.30; Nov-Mar, daily 11.00-16.00; closed 25/26 and 1/2 Jan; last entry 30 mins before closing.

Tel: 01470 521206   Web: www.dunvegancastle.com

Dunyvaig Castle

[Map: 91; H2] Off A846, 2 miles E of Port Ellen, Lagavulin, Islay. (NGR: NR 406455 LR: 60)

In a peaceful spot by the sea and opposite Lagavulin Distillery, Dunyvaig Castle is now very ruinous. All that remains are the ruins of a small 15th-century keep on top of a rock, with an inner and larger outer courtyard of the 13th century.

 There was a stronghold here from early times. The castle belonged to the MacDonald Lord of the Isles, who had their main stronghold at Finlaggan, also on Islay. The Lord of the Isles was forfeited by James IV in 1493, and passed to the MacIans, back to the MacDonalds and then to the Campbells. It was besieged and changed hands several times in the 17th century. The Campbells occupied the castle until about 1677, but demolished much of it soon afterwards, and moved to Islay House.

Parking nearby.

Access at all reasonable times – care should be taken.

Earl's Palace, Birsay (HS)

[Map: 92; A5] Off A966, 12 miles N of Stromness, Birsay, Orkney. (NGR: HY 248279 LR: 6)

Once a fine and stately building, the Earl's Palace at Birsay is a ruinous 16th-century courtyard castle, started by Robert Stewart, Earl of Orkney about 1574 and completed by his son, Patrick Stewart, before 1614. Father and son oppressed the islanders, and taxed them to pay for the palace at Birsay and at Kirkwall. Earl Patrick was charged with treason and executed in 1615 after his son, Robert Stewart, had risen against the Crown. Robert shared the fate of his father. The building was badly damaged in a gale of 1868.

Parking nearby

Access at all reasonable times.

Tel: 01856 721205/841815

Earl's Palace, Kirkwall (HS)

[Map: 93; A6] On A960, W of Kirkwall, Orkney. (NGR: HY 449107 LR: 6)

By the Bishop's Palace and Cathedral and an unusual and formerly lavish edifice, the Earl's Palace is a ruinous U-plan palace, dating from the 17th century. It consists of a main block, one long projecting wing, and another small offset square wing. The building is dominated by large oriel windows.

The palace was built by Patrick Stewart, Earl of Orkney, the illegitimate half-brother of Mary, Queen of Scots. He oppressed the Orcadians, and was imprisoned in 1609. His son led a rebellion in the islands in 1614, capturing the Palace and Kirkwall Castle, as well as Earl's Palace at Birsay. The rising was put down, and Patrick and Robert Stewart were both executed in Edinburgh in 1615. The Bishops of Orkney occupied the palace until 1688. (Also see Bishop's Palace). The fine medieval cathedral stands nearby.

Explanatory displays. Parking nearby. £. Joint entry ticket for all Orkney monuments available.
Open Apr-Sep, daily 9.30-18.30, last entry 30 mins before closing.
Tel: 01856 871918

Edinburgh Castle (HS)

[Map: 94; H5] Off A1, in the centre of Edinburgh. (NGR: NT 252735 LR: 66)

Located on a high rock above the capital, Edinburgh Castle was one of the strongest and most important fortresses in Scotland. The oldest building is a small Norman chapel of the early 12th century, dedicated to St Margaret, wife of Malcolm Canmore, who died at the castle in 1097. The castle was built and rebuilt down the centuries and is an impressive complex of building with fine views over the capital. The castle is the home of the Scottish crown jewels, and the Stone of Destiny, on which the Kings of Scots were inaugurated from earliest times. Among the many other attractions, there is also the magnificent cannon Mons Meg, the Scottish War Memorial and the Regimental Museum of the Royal Scots.

The castle had an English garrison from 1296 to 1313, when the Scots climbed the rock, surprised the garrison, and retook it. The castle was slighted, but there was an English garrison here again until 1341, when it was retaken by a Scottish force disguised as merchants. In 1367-71 David II rebuilt the castle with strong curtain walls and towers, and a large L-plan keep, David's Tower, which was named after him. After the murder of the young Earl of Douglas and his brother at the 'Black Dinner' at the castle in 1440, it was attacked and captured by the Douglases after a nine-month siege, and required substantial repairs. In 1566 Mary, Queen of Scots, gave birth to the future James VI in the castle. After her abdication, it was held on her behalf, until English help forced it to surrender in 1573. The castle was captured in 1640 after a three-month siege by the

Covenanters, and Cromwell besieged it throughout the autumn of 1650. The Jacobites failed to take it in both the 1715 and 1745 Risings. Many of the present buildings date from the 17th and 18th centuries. The castle is reputedly haunted by several ghosts, including a headless drummer seen in 1960, a ghostly piper who disappeared searching a passageway beneath the castle, and the spectre of a dog whose remains are buried in the pet's cemetery.

Explanatory displays. Audio-guide tour. Guided tours. Gift shop. Restaurant. WC. Disabled access. Visitors with a disability can be taken to the top of the castle by a courtesy vehicle; ramps and lift access to Crown Jewels and Stone of Destiny. Car and coach parking (except during Tattoo). £££.

Open all year: Apr-Sep, daily 9.30-18.00; Oct-Mar, daily 9.30-17.00; last entry sold 45 mins before closing; times may be altered during Tattoo and state occasions; closed 25/26 Dec; open 1/2 Jan: tel for opening hours.

Tel: 0131 225 9846

Edzell Castle (HS)

[Map: 95; F6] Off B966, 6 miles N of Brechin, Edzell, Angus. (NGR: NO 585693 LR: 44)

Edzell is an attractive and stately castle, although now ruinous, and consists of an early 16th-century tower house, later enlarged and extended with ranges of buildings around a courtyard. A notable feature is the large pleasance, or garden, which was created in 1604. It is surrounded by an ornamental wall, to which a summerhouse and a bath-house were added. The fine carved decoration of the garden walls is unique, and the garden is laid out with formal parterre.

The castle was built by the Lindsay Earls of Crawford. Mary, Queen of Scots, stayed here in 1562, and Cromwell garrisoned Edzell in 1651. The Lindsays had to sell the property in 1715, because of huge debts, and it was bought by the Maule Earl of Panmure. One story associated with the castle is that the one of the Lindsay lairds was cursed by a gypsy woman, after he had hanged her sons for poaching. The tales goes that his pregnant wife died that day, while he himself was devoured by wolves. The castle is also said to be haunted by Catherine Campbell, wife of David, 9th Earl of Crawford. She had apparently died and had been interred at the family vault. A sextant tried to steal her rings, but she had been in a coma and this roused her. Her ghost, a 'White Lady', is said to haunt the ruins and the burial ground of Edzell Old Church, which has the Lindsay Burial Aisle.

Visitor centre. Exhibition and explanatory panels. WC. Garden. Picnic area. Reasonable disabled access and WC. Car and coach parking. Group concessions. £.

Open all year: Apr-Sep, daily 9.30-18.30; Oct-Mar, Sat-Wed 9.30-16.30, closed Thu & Fri; last entry 30 mins before closing; closed 25/26 Dec and 1/2 Jan.

Tel: 01356 648631

Eilean Donan Castle

Eilean Donan Castle

[Map: 96; E3] On A87, 8 miles E of Kyle of Lochalsh, Dornie, Highland. (NGR: NG 881259 LR: 33)

One of the most beautifully situated of all Scottish castles, Eilean Donan Castle consists of a 13th-century wall, surrounding a courtyard, with a strong 14th-century keep. Adjoining ranges of out-buildings and fortifications were added in later centuries. Although very ruinous, it was completely rebuilt in the 20th century, and it stands in a strategic and picturesque spot at the mouth of Loch Long and Loch Duich.

Alexander III gave the lands to Colin Fitzgerald, son of the Irish Earl of Desmond and Kildare, for his help in defeating King Hakon and his Norsemen at the Battle of Largs in 1263. The family changed their name to Mackenzie, and Eilean Donan became their main stronghold. Robert the Bruce sheltered here in 1306. In 1331 Randolph, Earl of Moray, executed 50 men at Eilean Donan and adorned

the castle walls with their heads, and in 1509 the MacRaes became constables of the castle. In 1539 it was besieged by Donald Gorm MacDonald, a claimant to the Lordship of the Isles, but he was killed by an arrow shot from the castle. William Mackenzie, 5th Earl of Seaforth, had it garrisoned with Spanish troops during the Jacobite rising of 1719, but three frigates battered it into submission with cannon, and it was blown up from within. The ghost of one of the Spanish troops, killed either at the castle or the nearby battle of Glenshiel, is said to haunt the castle; as does the ghost of Lady Mary, witnessed in one of the bedrooms. There are mementoes of Bonnie Prince Charlie and James VIII and III; and the film has been used in many movies, including the James Bond film 'The World is Not Enough', 'Highlander' with Christopher Lambert and Sean Connery, 'Loch Ness' with Ted Danson, as well as the TV series 'The Avengers'.

Guided tours available. Visitor centre. New exhibitions. Gift shop. Tearoom. WC and disabled WC. Car and coach parking. Group concessions. ££.

Open Mar-Nov, daily 10.00-17.30; may also be open in winter: check with castle.

Tel: 01599 555202   Web: www.eileandonancastle.com

Elcho Castle (HS)

[Map: 97; G5] Off A912, 4 miles E of Perth, Elcho, Perthshire. (NGR: NO 165211 LR: 58)

In a pleasant location to the south of the River Tay, Elcho Castle is an impressive building, both stronghold and comfortable residence. The castle consists of a long rectangular main block and several towers. There is a fine quarry garden behind the building. The hall, on the first floor, has some remains of plasterwork and a large fireplace.

William Wallace is said to have sheltered here, but nothing of this early castle apparently remains. The Wemyss family held the property from 1468, and were made Lords Elcho, as well as Earls of Wemyss in 1633. David, Lord Elcho, fought and survived Culloden on the Jacobite side in 1746, but had to flee to France. By the 1780s, Elcho Castle was abandoned and fell into decay, but it was reroofed in 1830.

Kiosk. Picnic area. WC. Parking. £.

Open Apr-Sep, daily 9.30-18.30; last ticket sold 30 mins before closing.

Tel: 01738 639998

Falkland Palace (NTS)

[Map: 98; G5] Off A912, 10 miles N of Kirkcaldy, Falkland, Fife. (NGR: NO 254075 LR: 59)

A fortified but palatial residence remodelled in Renaissance style, Falkland Palace consisted of ranges of buildings around an open courtyard. The late 15th-century gatehouse range survives complete, while an adjoining range is ruined, and only traces remain of the range opposite the gatehouse. The last side was completed by a wall. There are extensive gardens and a real tennis court, which dates from 1539.

The Chapel Royal, with fine mullioned windows, has a 16th-century oak screen at one end, and the painted ceiling dates from 1633. There is also a fine tapestry gallery, and access to the keeper's apartments. The restored cross house contains a refurbished room, reputedly the King's Room, where James V died in 1542.

Falkland was used as a hunting seat by the kings of Scots from the 12th century. The property was owned by the MacDuff Earls of Fife, and the castle was sacked by the English in 1337. In 1371 it passed to Robert Stewart, Duke of Albany, and he had David, Duke of Rothesay, his nephew and the heir of Robert III, imprisoned and starved to death at Falkland in 1402. It became a favourite residence of the Stewart kings, and was used and remodelled by James III, James IV, and James V. Mary, Queen of Scots, visited the palace in 1563, James VI stayed at Falkland, as did Charles I in 1633, and Charles II in the 1650s. Rob Roy MacGregor was based here in 1716 during the Jacobite Rising. Despite a visit by George IV in 1822, the palace deteriorated until 1887 when it was restored by the 3rd Marquis of Bute. In 1952 The National Trust for Scotland assumed responsibility for the building.

Fasque

The Tapestry Gallery is said to be haunted by a 'White Lady', whose apparition is reputed to walk the length of the chamber before passing through a wall.

Explanatory displays. Gift shop. Visitor centre. Picnic area. Extensive gardens. Real tennis court. WC. Disabled access. Tape tour for visually impaired. Car parking nearby. ££.

Palace, garden and Town Hall open Mar-Oct, Mon-Sat 10.00-18.00, Sun 13.00-17.30; last entry 60 mins before closing.

Tel: 01337 857397

Fasque

[Map: 99; F6] Off B974, 5 miles NW of Laurencekirk, Kincardine and Deeside.
(NGR: NO 648755 LR: 45)

Fasque is a grand castellated mansion, started in 1809, and consists of a tall central tower of four storeys, and a three-storey main block and lower wings.

The lands were long held by the Ramsays, who had a castle, but passed to the Gladstones in 1829, one of whom, William Ewart Gladstone, was Prime Minister four times between 1830 and 1851. The house is said to be haunted by the ghost of Helen Gladstone, youngest sister of the Prime Minister, as well as the spirit of a butler called MacBean.

William Gladstone library, state rooms, kitchen, extensive domestic quarters and family church. WC. Picnic area. Deer park with Soay sheep and walks. Car and coach parking. ££.

Open only for organised groups of 12 or more by appt only.

Tel: 01561 340569   Web: www.fasque.com

Fast Castle

[Map: 100; H6] Off A1107, 6 miles NW of Eyemouth, Borders. (NGR: NT 862710 LR: 67)

Standing on a dizzying cliff-top promontory above the sea, Fast Castle is now very ruinous but there are some remains of a 15th-century keep and courtyard, which was once approached by a draw-bridge over the steep chasm.

It was occupied by the English after the Battle of Neville's Cross in 1346, but was recaptured by the Scots in 1410. Margaret Tudor stayed here in 1502. After destruction by the Duke of Albany in 1515, the castle was rebuilt by the Homes six years later. It was taken by the English around 1547, recovered by the Scots before 1566 when Mary, Queen of Scots stayed here, but was recaptured by the English in 1570. In 1580 it went to the Logans of Restalrig, but was ruinous after their forfeiture in 1600, and was later owned by the Douglases, Homes, Arnots and the Halls. It was reputedly used by smugglers, and there was a 'secret' cave below the old castle. There are also tales of treasure having been buried here, possibly hidden by Sir Robert Logan of Restalrig, who died in 1606.

Car parking nearby.

Access at all times – visit involves walk and care must be taken (joined to the 'mainland' by a gangway).

Ferniehirst Castle

[Map: 101; I6] Off A68, 1.5 miles S of Jedburgh, Borders. (NGR: NT 653179 LR: 80)

Ferniehirst Castle is an extended and altered tower house, which incorporates the cellars from the 16th-century castle, along with later wings and extensions. The original entrance leads to a stair known as the 'Left-Handed Staircase'. The story is that when Sir Andrew Kerr, who was himself left-handed, returned from Flodden in 1513 he had his followers trained to use their weapons with their left hands. This is said to be the origin of 'Corrie-fisted' or 'Kerr-handed'.

The castle was taken and sacked by the English in 1523, but was recaptured with French help in 1549, and the leader of the English garrison beheaded. Sir Thomas Kerr, protector of Mary, Queen of Scots, invaded England in 1570, hoping to have her released, but all that resulted was a raid on Scotland, during which Ferniehirst was damaged. James VI attacked the castle in 1593, because of help given by the family to the Earl of Bothwell, and the castle was rebuilt about 1598. It is still held by the family, and is said to be haunted by a 'Green Lady'.

Collection of portraits. Turret library. Guided tours. Explanatory displays. Gift shop. WC. Riverside walk. Sheep of Viking origin. Car and coach parking. £.

Open Jul, Tue-Sun 11.00-16.00.

Tel: 01835 862201

Finlaggan

[Map: 102; H2] Off A846, 3 miles W of Port Askaig, Loch Finlaggan, Islay. (NGR: NR 388681 LR: 60)

Finlaggan was a very important site in medieval times, but not much remains except foundations on two islands. The ruins of a chapel, dedicated to St Finlaggan a contemporary of St Columba, and many other buildings stand on the larger island, Eilean Mor. There are several carved gravestones, thought to commemorate relatives of the Lords of the Isles, who were themselves buried on Iona.

Somerled forced the Norsemen from much of western Scotland, but he was assassinated at Renfrew in 1164 when at war with Malcolm IV. Somerled was succeeded by his sons Reginald in Kintyre and Islay; Dugald in Lorn, Mull and Jura; and Angus in Bute, Arran and North Argyll. The whole area became part of the kingdom of Scots in 1266. Angus Og MacDonald (Young Angus) was the grandson of Donald, a son of Reginald: hence MacDonald the clan name. Angus was a friend and supporter of Robert the Bruce, and died at Finlaggan in 1328: his son, John of Islay, was the first to use the title 'Lord of the Isles'. The power, influence and independence of the Lords brought them into conflict with the kings of Scots. A campaign by the 2nd Lord led to the bloody Battle of Harlaw in 1411, and the 3rd Lord was twice imprisoned by James I. James IV eventually destroyed their power in a campaign in 1493 and the last Lord was imprisoned in Paisley Abbey. The island eventually went to the Campbells.

Visitor centre. Parking nearby.

Open Apr, Sun, Tue & Thu, 13.00-16.30; May-Sep, daily 13.00-16.30; Oct, Sun, Tue & Thu 13.00-16.00.

Tel: 01496 810629   Web: www.islay.com/sites/finlaggan.htm

Finlarig Castle

[Map: 103; G4] Off A827, 0.5 miles NE of Killin, W end of Loch Tay, Stirlingshire.
(NGR: NN 575338 LR: 51)

On a hillock in an atmospheric wooded setting, Finlarig Castle is a ruinous 17th-century Z-plan tower house. Two ruined square towers with shot-holes survive, and a passage leads past two cellars to the kitchen.

The lands were held by the Menzies family, but the castle was built in 1621-9 by the 'Black Duncan of the Cowl' or 'Black Duncan of the Castles' Campbell. Rob Roy MacGregor visited in about 1713. Parliament was summoned to appear here in 1651, but only three members turned up. Close by is said to be a beheading pit, containing a block and a sunken cavity for the head. Noble folk were executed in the pit, while the common people were hanged on a neighbouring oak tree. The pit may in fact be a water collection tank (or perhaps a cess pit) – but this does not make such a good story. This branch of the family became Earls of Breadalbane. There are the remains of a mausoleum close by.

Access at all reasonable times: view from exterior as dangerously ruined.

Finlaystone House

[Map: 104; H4] On A8, 5.5 miles E of Greenock, Renfrewshire. (NGR: NS 365737 LR: 63)

Overlooking the Clyde and set in fine gardens and woodland, Finlaystone House is a grand symmetrical mansion, mostly dating from 1760 and later, although remodelled between 1898 and 1903. The building incorporates a 15th-century castle, a property of the Cunningham Earls of Glencairn. Alexander, 5th Earl, had John Knox preach here in 1556, and opposed Mary, Queen of Scots, at the 'battle' of Carberry Hill in 1567. The 9th Earl led a rising for Charles II against Cromwell in 1654. Although the rebellion was a failure and he only just escaped execution, after the Restoration the Earl was made Chancellor of Scotland. Robert Burns – whose patron was James, 14th Earl – visited the house, and scratched his name on a window pane with his diamond ring. He also wrote a lament for the earl, and called his son James Glencairn Burns. The property later passed to the MacMillans, and there is a visitor centre with Clan MacMillan exhibits.

Visitor centre with Clan MacMillan exhibits, doll museum, and Celtic art display. Gift shop. Tearoom. WC. Gardens. Disabled access to grounds & WC. Parking. £.

House not open; gardens and grounds open all year, daily 10.30-17.00; visitor centre and refreshments open Apr-Sep, daily 11.00-17.00.

Tel: 01475 540505   Web: www.finlaystone.co.uk

Floors Castle

[Map: 105; H6] Off A6089, 1 mile NW of Kelso, Floors, Borders. (NGR: NT 711346 LR: 74)

Set in parkland near the River Tweed, Floors Castle consists of a large towered and turreted central block with other wings and ranges, and is the largest inhabited mansion in Scotland. The building dates from 1721, although there was an older house or castle; and was designed by William Adam for John Kerr, 1st Duke of Roxburghe. In the 19th century the house was remodelled with a profusion of spires and domes, corbelling and battlements, by William Playfair. It is still the home of the Duke and Duchess of Roxburghe, and was used in the film 'Greystoke'. There is a walled garden with fine herbaceous borders.

Collections of furniture, tapestries, works of art and porcelain. Gift shop. Licensed restaurant. WC. Playground. Walled garden and park. Disabled access to house; lift for wheelchairs; WC. Car and coach parking. Group concessions. £££.

Open mid Apr-mid Oct, daily 10.00-16.30; last entry 30 mins before closing.

Tel: 01573 223333   Web: www.floorscastle.com

Fyvie Castle (NTS)

[Map: 106; D6] Off A947, 8 miles S of Turriff and 1 mile N of Fyvie village, Fyvie, Banff & Buchan. (NGR: NJ 764393 LR: 29)

Standing by the River Ythan in fine gardens and policies, Fyvie is a huge and magnificent castle. There is a massive tower house with very long wings, which is adorned with turrets, dormer windows, carved finials and corbiestepped gables. There are fine original interiors, including wood panelling, plasterwork and painted ceilings, while the main turnpike stair is decorated with 22 coats of arms.

William the Lyon held court at Fyvie in 1214, as did Alexander II eight years later. Edward I of

England stayed in 1296, then Robert the Bruce in 1308. Fyvie was held by the Lindsays but was destined to have a succession of owners, and passed to the Prestons in 1402, then about 1433 to the Meldrums, then the Seton Earls of Dunfermline in 1596, the first of whom, Sir Alexander, was Chancellor of Scotland. The Marquis of Montrose occupied the castle in 1644, and in the 1650s it was held by a Cromwellian force. The property passed to the Gordon Earls of Aberdeen in 1733 and finally to the Leith family in 1889. It is now in the care of The National Trust for Scotland. Among many items of interest are the 'weeping stones' of Fyvie, which are said to exude water when tragedy is to come. The castle also has several ghost stories. It is said to be haunted by a 'Green Lady', the apparition of Lilias Drummond, wife of Sir Alexander Seton, and she died in 1601. Seton married within a few months, and the ghost is said to have carved its name D[ame] LILLIES DRUMMOND on the outside of the window sill of the newlyweds' bedroom – and the carving can still be seen (in what is now known as the Drummond Room). The castle also has tales of a 'Grey Lady', the spirit of a woman starved to death here; and of a spectral drummer or trumpeter, heard or witnessed as a herald of misfortune.

Collections of portraits, arms and armour and tapestries. Gift shop. Tearoom. WC. Picnic area. Garden and grounds. Plant sales. Disabled access to tearoom and WC. Car parking. £££

Open Apr-Sep: Apr-Jun & Sep, Sat-Wed 12.00-17.00, last entry 30 mins before closing; Jul-Aug, daily 11.00-17.00; grounds open all year, daily 9.30-sunset.

Tel: 01651 891266

Gilnockie Tower

[Map: 107; 16] Off A7, 9 miles N of Gretna, 2 miles N of Canonbie, Hollows Village, Dumfries and Galloway. (NGR: NY 383787 LR: 85)

Situated on a strong site, Gilnockie Tower is a rectangular 16th-century tower house of four storeys and a garret. It was a stronghold of the unruly Armstrong clan after an earlier tower had been destroyed by the English in 1523. Johnie Armstrong of Gilnockie was hanged without trial by James V in 1530, with 50 of his family. The tower has been rerooted and restored, and is now occupied by the Clan Armstrong Centre.

Guided tour. Explanatory displays. Gift shop. WC. Car parking. Group concessions - groups must book in advance. £

Open Apr-Oct, guided tour 14.30 onwards; other times by appt.

Tel: 01387 371876   Web: www.armstrong-clan.co.uk

Girnigoe Castle

[Map: 108; B5] Off A9, 3 miles N of Wick, Caithness, Highland (NGR: ND 379549 LR: 12)

Standing on a rocky promontory on cliffs above the sea, Girnigoe Castle and Castle Sinclair were two separate fortresses, although they stand very close together. Not much remains of Castle Sinclair, while Girnigoe consists of a ruinous keep with a main block and two projecting wings.

In 1472 the Sinclair Earls of Orkney were forced to resign the earldom and were given Caithness and Ravenscraig as compensation. The 2nd Earl, William, built a castle here but died at the Battle of Flodden in 1513. In 1571 George, 4th Earl, had John, Master of Caithness, his son and heir, imprisoned in the dungeons for seven years. The Master was fed on salted beef, and denied water so that he died mad with thirst. Cromwell had the castle garrisoned in the 1650s, and the castle was damaged when the Campbells attempted to seize the earldom in 1679. The property passed to the Dunbars of Hempriggs, but was sold back to the Sinclairs about 1950, and is now held in trust.
Car parking.

Access at all reasonable times: medium walk to site – view from exterior and great care should be taken.

Glamis Castle

[Map: 109; G6] Off A94, 5.5 miles SW of Forfar, 1 mile N of Glamis village, Angus.
(NGR: NO 387481 LR: 54)

Lying in extensive parkland with a garden and pinetum, Glamis Castle is a massive castle and stately home. At its core is a greatly extended keep, dating from the 14th century, and later altered to an L-plan and with a large round stair-tower. The keep was heightened, and the battlements replaced by turrets and dormers. It was extended again, with lower wings and round towers in the following centuries. There is a wide turnpike stair rising 143 steps from the basement to the battlements.

The predecessor of Glamis was reputedly intended to be built on the Hill of Denoon in the 11th century. The area was supposedly the domain of supernatural beings, and the foundations of the castle were repeated cast down, until it was decided to build the stronghold at its present site. Glamis is traditionally associated with Macbeth, and in the old keep is 'Duncan's Hall', but any connection is probably only based on Shakespeare's play. The lands were held by the Lyon family, who were made Lords Glamis in 1445.

Janet Douglas, beautiful widow of John Lyon, 6th Lord Glamis, was sister of the Earl of Angus; and was consequently hated, along with her family, by James V. James's spite led to Janet being accused of both trying to poison the king as well as on a dubious charge of witchcraft. The poor woman acted with great dignity and bravery, but had no way of escaping James's wrath, she was burned to death on Castle Hill in Edinburgh on 3 December 1537. Her apparition, the 'Grey Lady of Glamis', is said to haunt the building, and has been witnessed in the chapel. Mary, Queen of Scots, stayed here in 1562. In 1578 the 8th Lord was killed in a brawl with the Lindsays in Stirling, and his brother was one of those involved in the kidnapping of the young James VI in the 'Raid of Ruthven'. The family were made Earls of Kinghorne in 1606, and then Earls of Strathmore in 1677. The castle is still held by them, and the Queen Mother, Elizabeth Bowes Lyon who died in 2002, came from this family.

The ghost of Alexander Lindsay, 4th Earl of Crawford, 'Earl Beardie', is said to haunt a walled-up room where he played cards with the devil. Other stories of ghosts and beasts abound and are widely reported, including that of the spirit of a little African boy, which (along with many other tales) appears to have no foundation.

Collections of historic pictures, porcelain and furniture. Guided tours. Three additional exhibition rooms. Four shops. Licensed restaurant. WC. Picnic area. Playpark. Extensive park, pinetum, nature trail and garden. Disabled access to gardens and ground floor; WC. Car and coach parking. Group concessions. £££.
Open Apr-Oct, daily 11.00-17.00, last tour 15.30; Jul-Aug, from 10.00; last admission 16.30; at other time groups by appt.
Tel: 01307 840393   Web: www.glamis-castle.co.uk

Glenbarr Abbey

[Map: 110; H3] On A83, 12 miles N of Campbeltown, Glenbarr, Kintyre, Argyll.
(NGR: NR 669365 LR: 68)
Glenbarr Abbey is a large sprawling mansion, and dates from the 18th-century. Built in the Gothic revival style, and designed by James Gillespie Graham, it has been the home of the lairds of Glenbarr since 1796. There are tours, which are conducted by the 5th laird, Angus MacAlister, who also owns the property. Items on display include china, a thimble collection, antique toys, jewellery, and gloves worn by Mary Queen of Scots. The fine grounds feature river-side and woodland walks.
Guided tours. Museum. Explanatory displays. Gift shop. Tearoom. Grounds. Woodland and riverside walk. Picnic facilities. WC. Car and coach parking. Group concessions. £.
Open Easter-Oct, daily 10.00-17.00; closed Tue.
Tel: 01583 421247   Web: www.kintyre-scotland.org.uk/glenbarr

Glenbuchat Castle (HS)

[Map: 111; E6] Off A97, 10 miles W of Alford, 4.5 miles W of Kildrummy, Aberdeenshire.
(NGR: NJ 397149 LR: 37)
Glenbuchat Castle is a roofless, but otherwise complete, late 16th-century Z-plan tower house. Round and square turrets crown the corners of the tower.

The castle was built by the Gordons. It was occupied by James VI's forces during the Catholic rebellion of the Gordon Earl of Huntly of 1592. Brigadier-General John Gordon of Glenbuchat fought for the Jacobites in both the 1715 and 1745 Risings, and led the Gordons and Farquharsons at the Battle of Culloden in 1746 – when already 70. He was hunted after the battle, but managed to escape to Norway disguised as a beggar, and died in France. The castle was a ruin by 1738, and later sold to the Duff Earl of Fife.
Parking nearby.
Access at all reasonable times.
Tel: 01667 460232

Greenknowe Tower (HS)

[Map: 112; H6] On A6105, 7 miles NW of Kelso, 0.5 miles W of Gordon, Borders.

(NGR: NT 639428 LR: 74)

Set near the road on a hillock, Greenknowe Tower is a compact L-plan tower house, dating from the 16th century and with turrets crowning the corners of the building. The entrance, in the re-entrant angle, still has the original iron yett. There are some old trees nearby.

Greenknowe passed by marriage from the Gordons to the Setons of Touch, who built the castle. In the 17th century it was acquired by the Pringles of Stichil and then the Dalrymples, and occupied until the middle of the 19th century.

Parking nearby in lay-by.

Access at all reasonable times.

Gylen Castle

[Map: 113; G3] Off unlisted track, 2 miles SW of Balliemore, Gylen, S side of Kerrera.
(NGR: NM 805265 LR: 49)

On a rocky promontory jutting into the sea on the peaceful island of Kerrera, Gylen Castle ('castle of fountains') is a small but elegant L-plan tower house of the 16th century. The main block rises to four storeys, while the wing rises a storey higher.

An earlier castle here may have been where Alexander II died during an expedition against the Norsemen to recover the Western Isles, although Dalrigh near Horse Shoe Bay is given as an alternative site. The existing castle, built by Duncan MacDougall, was completed in 1582, but was burnt by a Covenanter army in 1647. The castle can be reached by foot and is some three miles from the ferry landing, and is currently being restored and consolidated.

Access at all reasonable times – care should be taken (take the Kerrera ferry from near Oban then three mile walk).

Haddo House (NTS)

[Map: 114; D6] Off B9005, 10 miles NW of Ellon, Haddo, Aberdeenshire. (NGR: NJ 868347 LR: 30)

Haddo House is a fine although somewhat plain classical mansion with two sweeping wings. It was built in 1731-6 and designed by William Adam for William Gordon, 2nd Earl of Aberdeen. The house was remodelled in the 1880s. Nothing survives of an old castle of the Gordons, who had held the lands from 1429.

In 1644 Sir John Gordon of Haddo, who had been active with the Marquis of Montrose, was captured after being besieged in the old castle for three days. He was imprisoned in 'Haddo's Hole' in St Giles Cathedral before being executed by beheading. The old castle was then destroyed. His son Sir George, however, became Lord Chancellor of Scotland and Earl of Aberdeen in 1684, while George, 4th Earl, was Prime Minister, although he resigned in 1854. The Gordons lived here well into the 20th century, and were made Marquesses of Aberdeen and Temair in 1915. There is a fine terraced garden and adjacent country park.

Generally guided tours, Mon-Sat. Exhibition of paintings. Explanatory displays. Gift shop. Restaurant. WC. Garden. Adjoining country park (01651 851489). Disabled access. Car and coach parking. Group concessions. £££

Open May-Jun, Sat-Sun 11.00-16.30, closed Mon-Fri; Jul-Aug, daily 11.00-16.30; Sep, Sat-Sun 11.00-16.30; closed some Sat in summer for events.

Tel: 01651 851440

Hailes Castle (HS)

[Map: 115; H6] Off A1, 4 miles E of Haddington, 1.5 miles W of East Linton, East Lothian. (NGR: NT 575758 LR: 67)

In a lovely and peaceful location above the River Tyne, Hailes Castle is a scenic ruin. It consists of a 14th-century keep, extended by ranges and towers in the following centuries, within a thick curtain wall. The castle had a large courtyard, fragments of which remain. It also has two pit prisons, one of which is said to be haunted by the ghost of a man starved to death. There are also tales of a underground tunnel linking the castle to Traprain Law.

Hailes was long a Hepburn property, later Earls of Bothwell, although the castle was seized in 1443, and the garrison and servants were slaughtered. The castle was burnt in 1532, and 15 years later was occupied for the English. James, 4th Earl of Bothwell brought Mary, Queen of Scots, here after abducting her in 1567, and they married soon afterwards. In 1650 the castle was partly disman-

Hermitage Castle

tled by Cromwell. It passed to the Stewarts, then the Setons, who in 1700 sold the castle to the Dalrymples of Hailes, but was then abandoned for the mansion of New Hailes, near Musselburgh. In 1835 Hailes was being used as a granary.

Picnic area. Parking.

Access at all reasonable times.

Hermitage Castle (HS)

[Map: 116; I6] Off B6399, 5 miles N of Newcastleton, Borders. (NGR: NY 494960 LR: 79)

Set a lonely and windswept location near the English Border, Hermitage is one of the most impressive and oppressive of Scottish fortresses. It consists of a solid 13th-century courtyard and large 14th-century keep of four storeys, around which has been constructed a massive castle.

The property belonged to the Dacres, but passed to the Soulis family. The story goes that one of the family (either Nicholas or his son William) was an evil warlock. Many local infants were seized by Soulis for use in his spells and never seen again. The local people eventually had Soulis wrapped in

lead and boiled in a cauldron until he melted. William, however, may actually have been imprisoned in Dumbarton Castle for plotting against Robert the Bruce. The family were certainly forfeited in 1320.

The castle passed to the Grahams of Abercorn, then by marriage to the Douglas family. William Douglas, 'The Knight of Liddlesdale', was prominent in resisting Edward Balliol in 1330s but seized Sir Alexander Ramsay of Dalhousie and starved him to death at Hermitage. In 1353 Douglas was murdered by his godson, another William Douglas, and in 1492 the castle was exchanged for Bothwell with the Hepburn Earls of Bothwell. James Hepburn, 4th Earl of Bothwell, was badly wounded in a skirmish with 'Little Jock' Elliot of Park (who was mortally wounded) in 1566, and was paid a brief visit by Mary, Queen of Scots, who rode all the way from (and then back to) Jedburgh. The property passed to Francis Stewart, Earl of Bothwell, then to the Scotts of Buccleuch in 1594. The castle was partly restored in the 19th century.

There are said to be several ghosts, including those of the evil Soulis, Alexander Ramsay of Dalhousie, and Mary, Queen of Scots.

Sales area. Picnic area. Car and coach parking. Group concessions. £.

Open Apr-Sep, daily 9.30-18.30, last entry 30 mins before closing.

Tel: 01387 376222

Hill of Tarvit Mansion House (NTS)

[Map: 117; G6] Off A916, 2.5 miles S of Cupar, Hill of Tarvit, Fife. (NGR: NO 380119 LR: 59)

Hill of Tarvit is a two-storey symmetrical mansion with small projecting bow-fronted wings. The original house dating from 1696 and designed by Sir William Bruce, with 19th-century wings, was virtually rebuilt in 1906 by Sir Robert Lorimer for Mr F. B. Sharp, a Dundee industrialist. Sharp wanted to house his fine collections of paintings and pictures, including works by Raeburn and Ramsay, furniture including Chippendale, Flemish tapestries and Chinese porcelain and bronzes. There are also fine formal gardens, also designed by Lorimer; and Scotstarvit Tower is close by.

Explanatory displays. Gift shop. Tearoom. Picnic area. Restored Edwardian laundry. Woodland walk. Scotstarvit Tower is nearby. Disabled access to ground floor and grounds suitable and WC. ££.

Open Easter or Apr-beg Oct, daily 13.00-17.00, last entry 45 mins before closing; shut some Sat for events; garden and grounds open all year, daily 9.30-sunset.

Tel: 01334 653127

Holyroodhouse, Edinburgh

[Map: 118; H5] Off A1, at foot of Royal Mile, in Edinburgh. (NGR: NT 269739 LR: 66)

Holyroodhouse consists of ranges of buildings surrounding a rectangular courtyard, one of which dates from the 16th century; and was built out of the guest house of the Abbey. The building was remodelled and extended by Sir William Bruce for Charles II in 1671-8. Original 16th-century interiors survive in the old block, and the ruins of the abbey church adjoin.

Holyrood Abbey was founded by David I around 1128. James III found the guest range of the abbey a comfortable alternative to Edinburgh castle, and James IV and James V extended the house. Part of the church became the Chapel Royal and is the burial place of David II, James V and Lord Darnley.

David Rizzio, the secretary Mary, Queen of Scots, was murdered in 1566 at the palace in her presence by men led by her husband, Lord Darnley, and a plaque marks the spot (he is buried in nearby Canongate Cemetery). Bonnie Prince Charlie stayed here for six weeks in 1745, and held court after the Battle of Prestonpans; while the Duke of Cumberland made it his residence after the Rising. The palace is the official residence of the monarch in Scotland. The State apartments house tapestries and paintings, and the Picture Gallery has portraits of over 80 kings of Scots (nearly all entirely from the imagination of the artist). The Queen's Audience Chamber is said to be haunted by a 'Grey Lady', and other ghostly manifestations have been reported.

Guided tours Nov-Mar. Gift shop. WC. Garden. Disabled access. Car and coach parking. Group concessions (10% groups of 15 or more). £££.

Open all year (except when monarch is in residence, Good Friday and 25/26 Dec): Apr-Oct, daily 9.30-18.00; Nov-Mar, daily 9.30-16.30; last entry 60 mins before closing.

Tel: 0131 556 1096/7371   Web: www.royal.gov.uk

Hopetoun House

[Map: 119; H5] Off A904, 6 miles E of Linlithgow, Hopetoun, West Lothian. (NGR: NT 089790 LR: 65)
Situated on the shores of the Firth of Forth in acres of parkland, Hopetoun House is a large and stately palatial mansion. It consists of a central block and flanking wings, and dates between 1699 and 1707, having been built by Sir William Bruce for the Hope family. Sir Charles Hope was made Earl of Hopetoun in 1703, then later Marquis of Linlithgow, and had the house remodelled by William Adam from 1721, the work being continued by John and Robert Adam. The house was transferred to a charitable trust in 1974. There are fine interiors, including paintings by famous artists, 17th-century tapestries, rococo ceilings and Meissen ceramics. The house is set in 100 acres of rolling parkland, including woodland walks, a red deer park, and a spring garden.

The house is said to have a harbinger of tragedy in the Hope family: the phantom of a man, clad in black and seen on a path near the house.

Fine interiors. Collections of furniture, tapestries and pictures. Gift shop. Restaurant. WC. Picnic area. Exhibitions. 100 acres of park land. Woodland walks. Red deer park. Croquet. Car and coach parking. Group concessions. ££.
Open daily Apr-Sep 10.00-17.30; last entry 60 mins before closing; other times closed except for group visits by prior appt.
Tel: 0131 331 2451   Web: www.hopetounhouse.com

House of Dun (NTS)

[Map: 120; F6] Off A935, 3 miles NW of Montrose, Angus. (NGR: NO 667599 LR: 54)
House of Dun, a fine classical mansion, was built in 1730 by William Adam for David Erskine Lord Dun. The house has fine plasterwork, and there is a miniature theatre display, as well as a small walled garden and extensive grounds. The lands had passed to the Erskines by 1375, and they had a castle. The castle was the scene of a notorious case of poisoning in 1613. The young John Erskine, heir to Dun, and his brother Alexander were poisoned by his

uncle, Robert Erskine, and his three aunts in a dispute over property. The older boy died in agony, while Alexander survived after a severe illness, and eventually succeeded to the lands. Robert Erskine and two of his sisters were executed.

Explanatory displays. Gift shop. Restaurant. Adventure playground. Fine plasterwork and a collection of portraits, furniture and porcelain. Walled garden and hand-loom weaving workshop. Woodland walk. Disabled access to ground floor and basement and WC. Info in Braille. £££.
House open Easter-Jun, Wed-Sun 12.30-17.30; Jul-Aug, daily 12.30-17.30; last entry 45 mins before closing; also Bank Hol Mons in the summer; grounds open all year, daily 9.30-sunset.
Tel: 01674 810264

Hume Castle

[Map: 121; H6] On B6364, 6 miles N of Kelso, Hume, Borders. (NGR: NT 704414 LR: 74)

Located in a prominent position with excellent views over the Tweed valley, Hume Castle was once a strong, strategic and important stronghold of the Home family. There was a castle here from the 12th or 13th century, which was thought to be impregnable before the development of gunpowder.

The lands were held by the Home family from the 13th century. The castle was captured by the English in 1547, although only after a stout resistance from the garrison led by Lady Home – her husband had been killed the day before in a skirmish before the Battle of Pinkie. In 1549 it was retaken by Lord Home, her son, and the English garrison was slaughtered. It was visited by Mary, Queen of Scots, in 1568, but the following year was again besieged by the English with artillery, and within 12 hours had surrendered. In 1650 the castle was surrendered Cromwell's forces, and was demolished. The family moved to The Hirsel, and the castle was not rebuilt. A folly was built on the foundations in 1794.

Explanatory displays. Car and coach parking.

Open all year, daily 9.00-21.00; in winter months, key available from the large house opposite castle.

Huntingtower Castle (HS)

[Map: 122; G5] Off A85, 2 miles NW of Perth, Huntingtower, Perthshire. (NGR: NO 083252 LR: 58)

Once known as Ruthven Castle, Huntingtower is an imposing and well-preserved castle. It consists of a 15th-century keep, a separate tower house dating from the next century, and a later small connecting range. Some of the old interior survives, including mural and ceiling painting and plasterwork, as well as decorative beams in the hall.

The property was held by the Ruthvens from the 12th century. Mary, Queen of Scots, visited the castle in 1565 while on honeymoon with Darnley, although the 3rd Lord Ruthven, Patrick, took part in the murder of Rizzio, Mary Queen of Scots's secretary. In 1582 William, 4th Lord Ruthven, who had been made Earl of Gowrie the previous year, kidnapped the young James VI – in what became known as the 'Raid of Ruthven' – and held him in Huntingtower for a year until the King escaped during a hunting trip. The Earl was beheaded in 1585. Fifteen years later John Ruthven, 3rd Earl of Gowrie, and his brother, Alexander, Master of Ruthven, were murdered at Gowrie House in Perth by James VI and his followers, in what is known as the 'Gowrie Conspiracy', a possible plot to murder the king. The Ruthvens were forfeited, their lands seized, and their name proscribed. The castle,

renamed Huntingtower, passed to the Murrays, later the Marquises and Dukes of Atholl. Lord George Murray, Bonnie Prince Charlie's general in the 1745-6 Jacobite Rising, was born here. The property was sold in 1805, and Huntingtower was used to house labourers.

The space between the battlements of the two towers is known as 'The Maiden's Leap'. Dorothy, daughter of the 1st Earl of Gowrie, is supposed to have jumped from one tower to the next. While visiting her lover, John Wemyss of Pittencrieff, in his chamber, and about to be discovered by her mother, she leapt to the other tower and returned to her own bed before being discovered. She eloped with her lover the following night.

The castle and grounds are said to be haunted by a 'Green Lady'. Her footsteps have reputedly been heard, along with the rustle of her gown, and she has reportedly appeared on several occasions, sometimes as a harbinger of death.

Gift shop. Picnic area. Car parking. Group concessions. £.

Open all year: Apr-Sep, daily 9.30-18.30; Oct-Mar, Sat-Wed 9.30-16.30, closed Thu & Fri; last ticket sold 30 mins before closing; closed 25/26 Dec and 1/2 Jan.

Tel: 01738 627231

Huntly Castle (HS)

[Map: 123; D6] Off A920, N of Huntly, Aberdeenshire. (NGR: NJ 532407 LR: 29)

A fine and sophisticated ruin with a long and turbulent history, Huntly Castle consists of a strong 15th-century keep, rectangular in plan with a large round tower at one end. The keep has oriel windows and fine fireplaces. There is an adjoining courtyard which had ranges of buildings on two sides, but these are now fragmentary.

An older castle here, called Strathbogie, was built by the MacDuff Earls of Fife on a nearby mound, and passed to the Gordons early in the 14th century. Robert the Bruce stayed here before defeating the Comyn Earl of Buchan at a battle nearby in 1307. This old castle was burned down in 1452, and a new castle was built close by. In 1506

the name was changed from Strathbogie to Huntly. George, 4th Earl, was defeated (and died, reportedly from apoplexy) by the forces of Mary, Queen of Scots, at Corrichie in 1562, and his son was executed. The castle was plundered.

The castle was restored, but in 1594 was attacked by James VI and damaged again after another rebellion by the then Earl, another George, only to be restored once again in 1602. In 1640 the castle was occupied by Covenanters, and four years later was taken by forces of the Marquis of Montrose. It was captured by General David Leslie in 1647 after starving out and slaughtering the garrison. George, 2nd Marquis of Huntly, was hanged for his support of Charles I two years later. It was held by Hanoverian soldiers, during the Jacobite rising of 1745-6; and The family were made Dukes of Gordon in 1864. By then it

had long been abandoned as a residence, and was used as a quarry and dump until cleared in 1923.
Exhibition. Gift shop. WC. Disabled WC. Parking. £.
Open all year: Apr-Sep, daily 9.30-18.30; Oct-Mar, Sat-Wed 9.30-16.00, closed Thu & Fri; last ticket sold 30 mins before closing; closed 25/26 Dec and 1/2 Jan.
Tel: 01466 793191

Inveraray Castle

[Map: 124; G4] Off A83, N of Inveraray, Argyll. (NGR: NN 096093 LR: 56)
By the mouth of the River Aray on Loch Fyne, Inveraray Castle is a substantial classical mansion with corner towers and turrets. It was started in 1744, and built for the Campbell Dukes of Argyll. It was remodelled by William and John Adam; and then again in 1877 after a fire. The castle, which is still the seat of the Dukes of Argyll, houses many interesting rooms, with collections of tapestries and paintings, and superb displays of weapons. Rob Roy MacGregor's sporran and dirk handle are on display. The Clan Room features information of special interest to members of Clan Campbell.

Nearby but now demolished was the 15th-century castle of the Campbell Earls of Argyll. James V visited in 1533, as did Mary, Queen of Scots, in 1562. Archibald, 5th Earl, led Mary's forces to defeat at the Battle of Langside in 1568, and was later Lord High Chancellor of Scotland. Archibald, 8th Earl, was made Marquis of Argyll in 1641. The castle was burnt three years later by the Marquis of Montrose. Archibald cooperated with the Cromwellian administration and was himself executed by beheading using the Maiden (an early guillotine) in 1661. The family were made Dukes in 1701. The old castle was demolished as part of the 3rd Duke of Argyll's rebuilding of the new mansion and town.
Guided tours. Collections of tapestries and paintings. Displays of weapons. Rob Roy MacGregor's sporran and dirk handle. Clan Room. Gift shop. Tea room. WC. Picnic area. Woodland walks. Disabled access to ground floor only. Car and coach parking. Group concessions. ££.
Open Apr-Oct: Apr, May & Oct, Mon-Thu and Sat 10.00-13.00 and 14.00-17.45, Sun 13.00-17.45, closed Fri; Jun-Sep, Mon-Sat 10.00-17.45, Sun 13.00-17.45; last admissions 12.30 and 17.00.
Tel: 01499 302203   Web: www.inveraray-castle.com

Inverlochy Castle (HS)

[Map: 125; F4] Off A82, 1.5 miles NE of Fort William, Inverlochy, Highland. (NGR: NN 120754 LR: 41)
Inverlochy Castle is a ruined 13th-century courtyard castle with a round tower at each corner, and was held by the Comyns of Badenoch. One of the towers is larger than the others, and is known as 'Comyn's Tower'. There were two entrances, opposite each other, which had portcullises.

The Comyns were destroyed by Robert the Bruce around 1308, and the castle was later held by the Gordons of Huntly. Major consolidation work has been undertaken.
Parking nearby.
Access at all reasonable times.

Kelburn Castle

[Map: 126; H4] Off A78, 2 miles S of Largs, Kelburn, Ayrshire. (NGR: NS 217567 LR: 63)
With fine views over the Clyde, Kelburn Castle is a tall Z-plan tower house, dating from the 16th century but to which has been added a large symmetrical mansion. Part may date from 300 years earlier, and the castle was extended in later years.

The Boyles held the lands of Kelburn from the 13th century, and fought at the battles of Largs in 1263 and at Bannockburn in 1314. John Boyle of Kelburn, a supporter of James III, was killed at the Battle of Sauchieburn in 1488, and another of the family was killed at Pinkie in 1547. The Boyles were made Lord Boyle in 1699, and Earls of Glasgow and Viscounts Kelburn in 1703, for helping persuade reluctant Jacobites to sign the Act of Union. They still hold the castle, making Kelburn one of the oldest houses continuously occupied by the same family. The grounds are a country centre, and there is walled gardens with rare shrubs and trees.

Guided tours of house. Explanatory displays. Gift shop. Licensed tea room. Cafe. WC. Picnic area. Riding centre open all year. Assault and adventure courses. Secret Forest. Disabled limited access and WC. Car and coach parking. Group concessions. ££ (+£ entrance to castle).

Castle open: Jul-1st week in Sep; daily tours 13.45, 15.00 and 16.15; other times by appt only. Country centre and gardens open: Easter-Oct, daily 10.00-18.00. Also grounds only open: Nov-Easter, daily 11.00-17.00.

Tel: 01475 568685/204 (castle)   Web: www.kelburncastle.com

Kellie Castle (NTS)

[Map: 127; G6] Off B9171, 4 miles N of Elie, Kellie, Fife. (NGR: NO 520052 LR: 59)

Kellie Castle is a tall and imposing 16th-century tower house, consisting of a three-storey main block and three large square towers which make the building E-plan. The Vine Room, on one of the upper floors, has a ceiling painted by De Witt, and there are fine plaster ceilings and painted panelling. There is a magnificent walled garden featuring a good collection of old fashioned roses and herbaceous plants which are organically cultivated.

An earlier castle here belonged to the Siwards, but the present castle was built by the Oliphants, who held the lands from 1360 until 1613, when the 5th Lord Oliphant had to sell the property. It was bought by Sir Thomas Erskine of Gogar, made Earl of Kellie in 1619, a favourite of James VI.

Kellie was abandoned in 1829, but in 1878 James Lorimer leased Kellie as an almost roofless ruin and proceeded to restore it. Robert Lorimer, his son, spent most of his childhood at Kellie, and was later a famous architect. In 1970 Kellie passed into the care of The National Trust for Scotland.

The building is reputedly haunted by the ghost of Anne Erskine, the story goes that she fell from one of the upstairs windows to her death.

Victorian nursery, old kitchen, and audio-visual show. Explanatory displays. Gift shop. Tearoom. Magnificent walled garden. WC. Disabled access to ground floor and grounds. Car park. ££.

Castle open Apr-Sep, daily 13.00-17.00; garden and grounds open all year, daily 9.30-sunset.

Tel: 01333 720271

Kilchurn Castle (HS)

[Map: 128; G4] Off A85, 2 miles W of Dalmally, Kilchurn, Argyll.
(NGR: NN 133276 LR: 50)

A picturesque and much photographed ruin in a beautiful location by Loch Awe, Kilchurn Castle is a ruinous courtyard castle of the 15th century. It consists of a rectangular keep, which was extended with ranges of buildings in the 16th century. The building was later remodelled for use as a barracks.

The lands originally belonged to the MacGregors, who may have had a castle here, but were acquired by the Campbells of Glenorchy, who built or rebuilt the stronghold. Kilchurn was strengthened by Black Duncan of the Seven Castles, Sir Duncan Campbell, at the end of the 16th century. The Campbells withstood a two-day siege in 1654 by General Middleton before he retreated before Cromwell's forces. The castle was inhabited by the Campbells until 1740 when they moved to Taymouth. It was garrisoned by Hanoverian troops in 1745, but was ruinous some 25 years later.

Accessible through gate off A85: see below though.

Open Apr-Sep: access to the public by boat only – regular sailings from Loch Awe Pier: tel to check if ferry operating.

Tel: 01838 200440/200449 (ferry co.)

Kildrummy Castle (HS)

[Map: 129; E6] Off A97, 10 miles SW of Alford, Kildrummy, Aberdeenshire. (NGR: NJ 454164 LR: 37)

Although now quite ruinous, Kildrummy Castle was one of the largest and mightiest early castles in Scotland, and remains a grand building in a fine location. It dates from the 13th century, and high curtain walls enclosed a courtyard with six round towers at the corners and gate. One of these, the largest, called 'The Snow Tower', may have been the main keep.

The castle was captured by Edward I of England in 1296, and then again five years later from a garrison led by Nigel, younger brother of Robert the Bruce, after the castle was set alight by a traitor. Nigel Bruce, and the rest of the garrison, were executed by hanging. The traitor was rewarded with much gold – poured molten down his throat.

The castle was restored before 1333, and besieged by the Earl of Atholl acting for the English two years later. It was successfully defended by Bruce's sister, Christian. Her husband, Sir Andrew Moray, the Regent, relieved the castle and killed the Earl of Atholl. David II besieged it in 1363, and seized it from the Earl of Mar. It passed to the Stewarts, then the Cochranes, then the Elphinstones, until they were compelled to give it to the Erskine Earls of Mar in 1626. It had been sacked in 1530 by the freebooter John Strachan of Lynturk; and was captured by Cromwell's forces in 1654.

The castle was badly damaged in 1690, when it was burned by Jacobites, but was complete enough

for 'Bobbing John' 6th Earl of Mar to use it as his base when he led the Jacobite Rising of 1715. After the collapse of the Jacobite cause, Kildrummy was deliberately dismantled, and then used as a quarry. *Gift shop. WC. Disabled WC. Parking. £.*
Open Apr-Sep, daily 9.30-18.30; last entry 30 mins before closing.
Tel: 01975 571331

Kinnaird Head Castle (HS)

[Map: 130; D7] Off A98, N of Fraserburgh,, Aberdeenshire. (NGR: NJ 999675 LR: 30)
Set on a rise looking out to sea, Kinnaird Head Castle consists of an altered massive keep, rectangular in plan and dating from the 15th century. The walls are harled and whitewashed; and the castle was a property of the Frasers of Philorth. Sir Alexander Fraser built the harbour at Fraserburgh (the town was formerly called Faithlie), came near to bankrupting himself, and had to sell much of his property in 1611. A lighthouse was built into the top of the castle in 1787, and the outbuildings were built around it in 1820 by Robert Stevenson, grandfather of Robert Louis Stevenson. It now forms part of Scotland's National Lighthouse Museum.

The Wine Tower, a lower tower, stands nearby, and has finely carved heraldic pendants adorning the upper vault. Sir Alexander Fraser is said to have had his daughter's lover, of whom he disapproved, chained in a sea cave below the building, where the poor man accidentally drowned. Fraser's daughter, Isobel, threw herself to her death on finding that her lover had been killed. An apparition is said to been seen by the Wine Tower whenever there is a storm.
Visitor centre with explanatory displays and audio-visual display. Gift shop. Tearoom. WC. Disabled access to museum and toilet. Car and coach parking. Group concessions. £.
Open daily all year as Lighthouse Museum, Apr-Jun & Sep-Oct, Mon-Sat 10.00-17.00, Sun 12.00-17.00; Jul-Aug, Mon-Sat 10.00-18.00, Sun 12.00-18.00; Nov-Mar, Mon-Sat 11.00-16.00, Sun 12.00-16.00; closed 25/26 Dec & 1/2 Jan – joint entry ticket.
Tel: 01346 511022

Kinross House Gardens

[Map: 131; G5] Off B996, E of Kinross, W side of Loch Leven, Perthshire. (NGR: NO 126020 LR: 58)
Kinross House, a large symmetrical mansion, is one of the finest examples of 17th-century architecture in Scotland. It was built by Sir William Bruce, who was Royal Architect to Charles II.

There was an earlier L-plan tower house, which was a property of the Douglases in the 16th century, but this was demolished in 1723. The property passed to the Bruces, then later to the Grahams. There are formal walled gardens with yew hedges, roses and herbaceous borders, which are open to the public.

Gift shop. Disabled access. Car parking. £.

House not open; gardens open Apr-Sep, daily 10.00-19.00.

Web: www.kinrosshouse.com

Kisimul Castle (HS)

[Map: 132; F1] Off A888, on island S of Castlebay, Barra. (NGR: NL 665979 LR: 31)

Defending Castle Bay to the south of Barra, Kisimul Castle has a curtain wall shaped to fit the island on which it stands, enclosing a keep, hall and other ranges of buildings, including a chapel.

Although Clan MacNeil claim descent from Neil of the Nine Hostages, High King of Ireland at the end of the 4th century, the first to settle in Scotland seems to have been Hugh, King of Aileachh and Prince of Argyll. His son, 21st in descent, was called Neil of the Castle, and built a stronghold here in 1030, or so it is claimed. One of its most unpleasant reputed occupants was Marion of the Heads, second wife of MacNeil of Barra, who ensured her own son's succession by beheading her stepsons. The clan were Jacobites, but only nominally, although even in 1750 an agent reported to the exiled Bonnie Prince Charlie that MacNeil of Barra would bring 150 men to a new rising in Scotland. The castle was abandoned around this time, and in 1795 was burnt out.

The 40th chief, Roderick, was forced to sell Barra in 1840 to the Gordons of Cluny, but the castle was bought back in 1937, and restored in the 1950s and 60s.

Parking nearby. £. Boat trip.

Open Apr-Sep, daily 9.30-18.30; last ticket 30 mins before closing.

Tel: 01871 810313

Lauriston Castle, Edinburgh

[Map: 133; H5] Off B9085, 3 miles W of Edinburgh Castle, Cramond Road South, Davidson's Mains, Edinburgh. (NGR: NT 204762 LR: 66)

Standing in fine and attractive grounds, Lauriston Castle is a 16th-century tower house, to which was added a two-storey Jacobean extension, designed by William Burn, in 1824-7. Two large pepper-pot turrets crown one side, and the castle has tall chimneys.

Leith Hall

The castle was built by the Napiers of Merchiston, and one of the family, John Napier, was the inventor of logarithms. In 1656 the property was sold and it passed through many hands until coming to the Reids in 1902, the last owners, who gave it to the city of Edinburgh. The castle has a fine Edwardian-period interior, housing good collections of Italian furniture, Blue John, Grossley wool mosaics, Sheffield plate, mezzotint prints, Caucasian carpets, and items of decorative art.

Good collections. Guided tours of house only. WC. Disabled access to grounds & WC. Japanese garden. Car and coach parking. Group concessions. ££ (castle).

Visit by guided tour only: Apr-Oct, Sat-Thu 11.20, 12.20, 14.20, 15.20 and 16.20, closed Fri; Nov-Mar, Sat-Sun only 14.20 and 15.20, closed Mon-Fri.

Tel: 0131 336 2060   Web: www.cac.org.uk

Leith Hall (NTS)

[Map: 134; D6] Off B9002, 8 miles S of Huntly, 3.5 miles NE of Rhynie, Leith Hall, Aberdeenshire. (NGR: NJ 541298 LR: 37)

Leith Hall is a fine building and incorporates a 17th-century rectangular tower house, with turrets crowning the corners. To this has been added 18th- and 19th-century blocks, to form four sides of a courtyard, with small drum towers at the corners. The walls are harled and yellow-washed; and there is a six-acre garden and woodland walks through the grounds.

The Leith family held the property from 1650 or earlier until 1945, when it was given to The National Trust for Scotland. There are Jacobite mementoes and an exhibition on the family's military history. Several ghosts are said to have been witnessed at Leith Hall, including the apparition of

a man with a bandaged head, a woman in Victorian dress, a young child and governess, and sounds as if a party was taking place.

Jacobite mementoes. Exhibition on family's military history. Exhibition. Tearoom. WC. Picnic area. Garden and 286 acres of extensive grounds with trails, ponds and a bird hide. Disabled facilities and WC. Car and coach parking. Group concessions. £££.

House and tearoom open Apr-Sep, Fri-Tue 12.00-17.00, last entry 45 mins before closing; garden and grounds open all year, daily 9.30-sunset.

Tel: 01464 831216

Lennoxlove

[Map: 135; H6] Off A1, between B6369 and B6368, 1 mile S of Haddington, Lennoxlove, East Lothian. (NGR: NT 515721 LR: 66)

Originally known as Lethington, Lennoxlove is an impressive altered L-plan keep tower house, which includes work from the 14th century, and probably earlier. A two-storey range projects from the tower, and there is another extension from the 17th century.

It was originally a property of the Giffords, but sold to the Maitlands about 1350, who built or

extended a castle here. It was burnt by the English in 1549. William Maitland of Lethington, secretary to Mary, Queen of Scots, lived here. He was involved in the plot to murder Lord Darnley, but supported Mary after she abdicated. He was taken prisoner after Edinburgh Castle was captured in 1573 and died, possibly by being poisoned, soon afterwards.

The property passed to the Maitland Duke of Lauderdale in 1645, but was sold to the Stewart Lord Blantyre. Instrumental in having the name changed to Lennoxlove was Frances Stewart, Duchess of Richmond and Lennox, a great beauty, who is said to have been the model for Britannia. It later passed to the Bairds, then in 1947 to the Duke of Hamilton, since when it has been the family seat. Among the treasures it contains are the death mask of Mary, Queen of Scots, a sapphire ring given to her by Lord John Hamilton, and the casket which may have contained the 'Casket Letters' . The 17th century part of the house contains the Hamilton Palace collection of pictures, furniture and porcelain, as well as the Nigel Tranter Centre..

Fully guided tours. Explanatory displays. Garden cafe. WC. Disabled access to house and gardens. Parking. ££.

Open Easter-Oct, Wed, Thu and Sun, 13.30-16.30; check if house is open on Sat before setting out; booked tours outwith these times by appt.

Tel: 01620 823720   Web: www.lennoxlove.org

Linlithgow Palace (HS)

[Map: 136; H5] Off A803, in Linlithgow, West Lothian. (NGR: NT 003774 LR: 65)
Once a splendid palace and still a fantastic ruin, Linlithgow Palace is located in the attractive burgh of Linlithgow by the shore of the loch. It consists of ranges of buildings set around a rectangular courtyard, and may include work from the 12th century. Stair-towers, within the courtyard, lead to all floors and the battlements, which run all round. There is a fine carved fountain in the courtyard, which has recently been restored.

There was a 12th-century castle here, which was captured and strengthened by Edward I of England in 1301, then known as the Peel of Linlithgow. It was slighted, after being retaken by the Scots by driving a cart under the portcullis; and remained a ruin until about 1350. It was repaired by David II, then mostly rebuilt by James I at the beginning of the 15th century. It became a favourite residence of Scottish monarchs, and the work continued under James III and James IV. Mary, Queen of Scots, was born here in 1542.

After the Union of the Crowns in 1603, the palace was left in charge of a keeper. It was last used by

Loch Doon Castle

Charles I in 1633 although his son, James, Duke of York, stayed here before succeeding to the throne in 1685. In the 1650s Cromwell had garrisoned the palace. It was also visited by Queen Anne with her father in the 1680s, Bonnie Prince Charlie in 1745 and the Duke of Cumberland. In 1746 General Hawley retreated here after being defeated by the Jacobites at the nearby Battle of Falkirk. The soldiers started fires to dry themselves, and the palace was accidentally set blaze. It was never restored.

The palace is said to be haunted by a 'Blue Lady', which has been witnessed walking from the entrance of the palace to the door of the nearby parish church of St Michael. Queen Margaret's bower, at the top of one of the stair-towers, is reputed to be haunted by the ghost of either Margaret Tudor, wife of James IV, or Mary of Guise, wife of James V (although neither of them seem very likely candidates).

It was in the parish church of St Michael that a blue-robed figure is said to have warned James IV not to invade England. James, of course, ignored the warning and was killed at the disastrous Battle of Flodden in 1513. The church is a fine building and is open to the public.

Explanatory panels and exhibition. Gift shop. WC. Picnic area. Disabled access. Car parking. Group concessions. ££.

Open all year: Apr-Sep, daily 9.30-18.30; Oct-Mar, daily 9.30-16.30; last ticket sold 45 mins before closing; closed 25/26 Dec and 1/2 Jan.

Tel: 01506 842896

Loch Doon Castle (HS)

[Map: 137; I4] Off A713, 7 miles S of Dalmellington, Ayrshire. (NGR: NX 483950 LR: 77)

In a remote spot on the west side of the loch, Loch Doon Castle is a ruinous 13th-century courtyard castle, polygonal in plan. A wall formerly enclosed ranges of buildings, including a 16th-century tower house. The castle originally stood on an island in the middle of the loch but, when the water level was raised by a hydroelectric scheme, the castle was moved to its present site, although (for some reason) the tower house was not rebuilt.

It was held by the Bruce Earls of Carrick, but was captured by the English in 1306. Sir Christopher Seton, Robert the Bruce's brother-in-law, was seized after the siege and then hanged at Dumfries. The castle was retaken by the Scots by 1314. In 1333 it was one of the six strongholds which held out for David II against Edward Balliol. It was gutted by fire in 1510 and, although restored, the castle was abandoned in the 17th century and became ruinous.

Parking.

Access at all reasonable times.

Lochleven Castle (HS)

[Map: 138; G5] Off B996, 1 mile E of Kinross, Loch Leven, Perthshire.
(NGR: NO 138018 LR: 58)

Standing on a sylvan island in the picturesque loch, Lochleven Castle is a small ruinous keep, rectangular in plan and dating from the 15th century. The keep is set at one corner of a courtyard, and the stronghold once occupied most of the island. The level of the loch has been lowered so that the island is now larger.

It was a royal castle from 1257, and was stormed by William Wallace after being captured by the English. The English, themselves, besieged the castle in 1301, but it was relieved by Sir John Comyn before it could be captured. It was visited by Robert the Bruce; and the castle was held again against Edward Balliol and the English in 1335. By the end of the 14th century, it had passed to the Douglases of Lochleven. Mary, Queen of Scots, was held here from 1567 until she escaped the following year, during which time she signed her abdication and is thought to have had a miscarriage. Her ghost is said to haunt the castle. The property passed to the Bruces of Kinross, then the Grahams, and the Montgomerys.

Gift shop. WC. Picnic area. Car parking at Kinross. ££.

Open Apr-Sep, daily 9.30-18.30; last ticket 30 mins before closing – includes boat trip from Kinross.

Tel: 07778 040483 (mobile)

Lochmaben Castle (HS)

[Map: 139; I5] Off B7020, 3 miles W of Lockerbie, Lochmaben, Dumfriesshire.
(NGR: NY 088812 LR: 78)

Once an important and powerful castle, Lochmaben Castle is now very ruinous. It dates in part from the 13th century, with a late keep and additions. It had a strong curtain wall, and was surrounded by a moat.

An older castle, of which only a motte survives, may be where Robert Bruce, later Robert I, King of Scots, was born. In 1298 Edward I of England chose a stronger site to build the castle. It was strengthened after being besieged by Robert the Bruce the following year, and it was attacked again by the Scots two years later. It was seized by Bruce in 1306, recovered by the English, but was finally surrendered to the Scots after Bannockburn in 1314.

It was held by the English from 1333 until 1384 when it was taken by Archibald the Grim, Douglas Lord of Galloway. In 1542 it was where the Scottish army was mustered by James V before going on to defeat at Solway Moss. Mary, Queen of Scots, and Darnley attended a banquet here in 1565. In 1588 James VI besieged and captured the castle from the Maxwells. The castle was then abandoned, and became ruinous.

Car parking

Access at all reasonable times – view from exterior.

Lochranza Castle

Lochranza Castle (HS)

[Map: 140; H3] Off A841, 10 miles N of Brodick, Lochranza, Arran. (NGR: NR 933507 LR: 69)
In a beautiful location by the sea, Lochranza Castle is a ruinous L-plan tower house. Much of the present building dates from the 13th or 14th century, but it was remodelled in the late 16th century. The main block rises to three storeys, with a higher wing capped by a watch-room.

Lochranza was used as a hunting lodge by the kings of Scots, and is said to have been visited by Robert the Bruce. The castle may have been built by the Stewarts of Menteith, the MacDonald Lord of the Isles or the Campbells, who appear to have held the property in 1315. It passed to the Montgomerys, later Earls of Eglinton, in 1452. James IV used it as a base to attack the MacDonald Lords of the Isles in the 1490s, and it was occupied by the forces of James VI in 1614 and then by Cromwell's troops in the 1650s. In 1705 it was sold to Anne, Duchess of Hamilton, but it had been abandoned by the end of the 18th century. It was recently sold again.
Car parking.
Key available locally.

MacLellan's Castle (HS)

[Map: 141; J4] On A711, in Kirkcudbright, Galloway. (NGR: NX 683511 LR: 83)
In the pleasant burgh of Kirkcudbright, MacLellan's Castle is a large and imposing ruinous L-plan tower house, which dates from the 16th century. It consists of a main block and a wing, a projecting rectangular tower, and two towers in the re-entrant angle. It is crowned by turrets, and the walls are pierced by gunloops.
    In 1569 Sir Thomas MacLellan of Bombie, Provost of Kirkcudbright, acquired the Franciscan Greyfriars Monastery, demolishing all but part of the chapel, now the Episcopalian Church, and built the castle about 1582. The MacLellans abandoned the castle around 1752, because of financial troubles, and it was sold to the Maxwells and then the Douglas Earl of Selkirk.
Sales area. Exhibition. WC. Parking. £.
Open Apr-Sep, daily 9.30-18.30; last entry 30 mins before closing.
Tel: 01557 331856

Manderston

[Map: 142; H6] Off A6105, 1.5 miles E of Duns, Manderston, Borders. (NGR: NT 810545 LR: 74)

Featuring the only silver staircase in the world, Manderston is a fine Edwardian mansion, and stands in acres of gardens and park land with woodland and lake-side walks. It includes work from the original house of 1790, when it was a property of the Homes, although there was an earlier house or castle here. Sir George Home of Manderston was involved in a witchcraft accusation involving his wife and Alexander Hamilton. The lady was cleared, but Hamilton implicated many others and himself, and he was executed in Edinburgh in 1630.

The house was virtually rebuilt between 1903-5 by John Kinross for Sir James Miller, a millionaire racehorse owner, whose family had acquired the property in 1890.

Fine interiors, above and below stairs. Museum. Tea room. WC. Gardens. 56 acres of park land. Woodland and lake-side walks. Car and coach parking. £££.

Open mid May-end Sep, Thu and Sun 13.30-17.00, last entry 45 mins before closing; Bank Holiday open Mon May and Aug, 13.30-17.00; other times group visits by appt; gardens open 11.30.

Tel: 01361 883450/882636   Web: www.manderston.co.uk

Mary Queen of Scots House

[Map: 143; I6] Off A68, in Jedburgh, Borders. (NGR: NT 651206 LR: 74)

Situated in a formal garden, Mary Queen of Scots House is an altered 16th-century T-plan tower house, consisting of a main block and a centrally projecting wing. A vaulted pend led to a courtyard, little of which remains.

The house belonged to the Scotts of Ancrum or the Kerrs. Mary, Queen of Scots, stayed in a chamber on the second floor. She was ill and lay near death for many days after her visit to the Earl of Bothwell at Hermitage Castle in 1566. She had ridden to the castle and back in the same day, and had fallen in a bog on the return journey. Above Mary's chamber is another similar room where the Queen's Four Marys are supposed to have stayed.

The building houses a museum displaying exhibits relating to the visit by Mary to Jedburgh.

Award-winning 16th-century house. Explanatory displays. Gift shop. Formal garden. WC. Disabled access to ground floor only. Parking nearby. £.

Open Mar-Nov, Mon-Sat 10.00-16.30, Sun 11.00-16.30.

Tel: 01835 863331   Web: www.scotborders.gov.uk/outabout/museums

Megginch Castle Gardens

[Map: 144; G5] About 8 miles E of Perth, E of A85, Megginch, Perthshire. (NGR: NO 242246 LR: 59)

Surrounded by woodlands, Megginch Castle is an altered L-plan tower house, with a 15th-century main block and a stair-wing dating from a century later. The building was later altered and extended. There are extensive gardens with 1000-year-old yews, 16th-century rose garden, kitchen garden, topiary and 16th-century physic garden.

Mellerstain

It was a property of the Hays, but was sold to the Drummonds of Lennoch in 1646. The 3rd Drummond of Megginch was the first member of Parliament for Perthshire for the Union parliament of 1707. Rob Roy MacGregor was imprisoned in Perth Tolbooth by Drummond, and part of the film 'Rob Roy' with Liam Neeson was made here. The Drummond family still live in the house.

Guided tours by arrangement and extra charge. Disabled partial access. Car and coach parking. £.

Castle not open; gardens open April-Oct, Wed 14.30-18.00, closed Thu-Tue; Jul, daily 14.30-17.00; other times by prior arrangement.

Tel: 01821 642222

Mellerstain

[Map: 145; H6] Off A6089, 5.5 miles NW of Kelso, Mellerstain, Borders. (NGR: NT 648392 LR: 74)

With lovely gardens and grounds, Mellerstain House is a magnificent castellated mansion, which was designed by William and Robert Adam. The wings date from 1725, while the central block was not completed until 1778, and replaced an earlier building. There are fine interiors.

The lands were held by the Halyburtons and others, but passed to the Baillies in 1642. Mellerstain was built for George Baillie of Jerviswood, and is now owned by the Baillie-Hamiltons, Earls of Haddington.

Collections of paintings and furniture. Fine interiors. Gift shop. Tearoom. Gardens and grounds. Disabled access to ground floor and grounds. Car and coach parking. £££.

Open Easter weekend (Fri-Mon), then May-Sep, daily except Tue & Sat 12.30-17.00, last entry 45 mins before closing; Oct, wknds only; groups at other times by appt; restaurant and grounds open, 11.30-17.30.

Tel: 01573 410225   Web: www.mellerstain.com

Menstrie Castle

[Map: 146; G5] Off A91, 5 miles NE of Stirling, 3 miles NW of Alloa, Castle Street, Menstrie, Clackmannan. (NGR: NS 852968 LR: 58)

Menstrie Castle consists of a small 16th-century L-plan tower house of two storeys and an attic, the wing of which was later greatly extended into a long block. It was a property of the Alexander family from around 1481. Sir William Alexander of Menstrie, 1st Earl of Stirling from 1587, was the founder of Nova Scotia, although he was later ruined and died bankrupt. The castle was burned by the Marquis of Montrose in 1645 because the family supported the Campbell Earl of Argyll. Menstrie passed to the Holbournes in 1649, one of whom was General James Holbourne, who fought against Cromwell at the Battle of Dunbar in 1650; then to the Abercrombies in 1719. The house was saved from demolition in the 1950s, and stands in a housing estate. A museum tells the story of Sir William, and the Nova Scotia Baronetcies.

Parking nearby.

Open Easter Sun, then May-Sep, Wed and Sun 14.00-17.00; administered by NTS and staffed by Clackmannanshire Council.

Tel: 01259 211701   Web: www.nts.org.uk

Mingary Castle

[Map: 147; F3] Off B8007, 1 mile E of Kilchoan, S coast of Ardnamurchan. (NGR: NM 502631 LR: 47)

In a beautiful location on the south coast of Ardnamurchan, Mingary Castle is a strong courtyard castle, with a high wall encircling the rock on which it stands and dating from the 13th century. Ranges were built within the walls.

Mingary was probably built by the MacIans of Ardnamurchan. It was occupied by James IV in 1493 and 1495 during his campaigns against the MacDonalds; and was demolished or slighted in 1517.

The MacIans supported the MacDonalds in the 1550s, and MacLean of Duart captured the chief of MacIan, then unsuccessfully besieged the castle with Spanish soldiers from an Armada galleon in Tobermory Bay. The Campbells, however, took Mingary from the MacIans. It was captured by Alaisdair Colkitto MacDonald in 1644 for the Marquis of Montrose, but was recaptured by the Covenanter General David Leslie two years later, then returned to the Argyll Campbells in 1651. The castle was garrisoned for the Government during the Jacobite Rising of 1745, and was probably still habitable around 1848. Although the building is fairly complete to the wallhead, it may be in a dangerous condition. The castle can be reached from along the shore from Kilchoan pier.

View from exterior.

Monzie Castle

[Map: 148; G5] Off A822, 2 miles NE of Crieff, Monzie, Perthshire. (NGR: NN 873245 LR: 52)

Monzie Castle is a large castellated mansion which incorporates a small L-plan tower house, much extended and remodelled in 1791. The tower is dated 1634, although it may incorporate work from the 16th century or earlier.

It was a property of the Scotts from the 15th century, then the Grahams (Graemes), then the Campbells until 1869, when it was sold to the Johnstones of Lathrisk. The house was restored around 1908 by Sir Robert Lorimer, after being burned out, and is now held by the Crichtons.

Parking. £.

Open mid May-mid Jun, daily 14.00-17.00; by appt other times.

Tel: 01764 653110

Morton Castle (HS)

[Map: 149; I5] Off A76, 2.5 miles NE of Thornhill, Morton, Dumfries and Galloway.
(NGR: NX 891992 LR: 78)

Built on a strong site by the banks of the loch, Morton Castle consists of a ruined 15th-century keep or altered hall-house, and a triangular courtyard, although little remains of two sides.

The property originally belonged to the Adairs, but passed to Sir Thomas Randolph early in the 14th century, then to the Earls of March, who built the existing castle. In 1459 it was acquired by the Douglases, later Earls of Morton, the most famous (or infamous) of whom was James Douglas, 4th Earl of Morton, Regent for James VI. He was executed in 1581 after being implicated in the plot to kill Darnley. The castle was occupied until about 1715.

Parking nearby

Access at all reasonable times – view from exterior.

Motte of Urr

[Map: 150; J5] Off B794, 2.5 miles NW of Dalbeattie, Urr, Dumfries and Galloway.
(NGR: NX 815647 LR: 84)

Motte of Urr is one of the best examples of a motte and bailey earthwork castle in Scotland, and dates from the 12th century, although the bailey may be even older and incorporate a hillfort. The site consists of a large 'pudding bowl' motte, defended by a ditch, within a raised oval bailey protected by another ditch, enclosing the motte.

It was a stronghold of the Lords of Galloway before they moved to Buittle in the 1240s. Devorgilla of Galloway, heiress of Allan, Lord of Galloway, married John Balliol whose son became John I of Scots. They were apparently very close and founded Balliol College, Oxford. She built Sweetheart Abbey, near Dumfries, where they are buried, and wore an amulet around her neck which contained Balliol's heart.

Parking nearby.

Access at all reasonable times.

Mount Stuart House

[Map: 151; H4] Off A844, 5 miles S of Rothesay, Mount Stuart, Bute. (NGR: NS 105595 LR: 63)

A fine Victorian Gothic stately home with splendid interior decoration, Mount Stuart was designed by the Scottish architect Robert Rowand Anderson for the 3rd Marquis of Bute. The house is surrounded by 300 acres of fine landscaped grounds, gardens and woodlands, and there is an octagonal glass pavilion with tropical plants. It was built on the site of an earlier house of 1719, designed by Alexander MacGill and later William Adam, which was burnt down in a disastrous fire in 1877.

Fine collection of family portraits. Visitor reception area. Guided tours. Gift shop. Tearoom. Picnic areas. Audio-visual presentation. WC. 300 acres of landscaped grounds, gardens and woodland. Glass pavilion with tropical plants. Adventure play area. Disabled facilities: access to house and most of gardens. Car and coach parking. Group concessions available. £££.

House and garden open Easter, then May-Sep, Sun-Fri 11.00-17.00, last tour 16.00; Sat, 10.00-14.30, last tour 13.30; gardens 10.00-17.00.

Tel: 01700 503877   Web: www.mountstuart.com

Moy Castle

[Map: 152; G3] Off A849, 10 miles SW of Craignure, Mull. (NGR: NM 616247 LR: 49)

In a lovely situation on a rocky crag by the seashore on the south coast of Mull, Moy Castle is a ruinous plain 15th-century keep of three storeys and a garret, remaining entire to the wallhead. Few castles are more beautifully sited.

The MacLaines owned the property. Iain the Toothless, the chief, and his son and heir, Ewen of the Little Head, fought in 1538 over the latter's marriage settlement. Ewen was slain in the subsequent battle, his head being hewn off and his horse riding away for two miles with the decapitated body. His ghost, the headless horseman, is said to been seen riding in Glen Mor on a dun-coloured horse, sometimes with a green cloak, when one of the MacLaines is about to die. MacLean of Duart, desiring Lochbuie, imprisoned the chief on the Treshnish Isle of Cairnburg to prevent him producing an heir. His only female companion was an old and ugly woman who, however, he contrived to make pregnant. MacLaine, himself, was murdered, but the woman managed to escape, and produced a son, who eventually regained the property. The castle was abandoned in 1752, and the MacLaines sold the property in the 20th century, although apparently retained possession of the castle.

Walk to castle.

View from exterior.

Mugdock Castle

[Map: 153; H4] Off A81, 8 miles N of Glasgow, Craigallian Road, 1.5 miles N of Milngavie, East Dunbartonshire. (NGR: NS 549772 LR: 64)

Standing in what is now a public park and formerly a large fortress of great strength, Mugdock Castle is now a ruin. It was a courtyard castle, and dated from the 14th century, but it was altered and extended as late as the 19th century.

It was a property of the Grahams from the middle of the 13th century. The most famous of the family was James Graham, 5th Earl and 1st Marquis of Montrose. Montrose led a brilliant campaign against the Covenanters in 1644-5 winning battles at Tippermuir, Aberdeen, Inverlochy, Auldearn, Alford, and Kilsyth, but was finally defeated by David Leslie at Philiphaugh. Montrose escaped to the continent where he distinguished himself, but returned in 1650 to be defeated at Carbisdale. He was captured and then hanged in Edinburgh, his body being put on display. The family was forfeited, and Mugdock was acquired the Campbell Marquis of Argyll. It was recovered by the Grahams in 1661 when Argyll, himself, was executed. Montrose was then given a splendid funeral and his remains placed in St Giles Cathedral in Edinburgh. The Grahams moved to Buchanan Castle in the 18th century. In 1875 a large castellated mansion was built in the ruins of the old castle, although this house has since been demolished and castle is quite ruinous.

Explanatory displays. Gift shop. Restaurant. Tearoom. Picnic and barbecue areas. WC. Play areas and walks. Craigend stables and bridle routes. Disabled access and WC. Tactile map. Car and coach parking.

Park open all year: summer 9.00-21.00; winter 9.00-17.30.

Tel: 0141 956 6100   Web: www.mugdock-country-park.org.uk

Muness Castle (HS)

[Map: 154; B7] Off A968, SE end of island of Unst, Muness, Shetland. (NGR: HP 629012 LR: 1)

Located on Unst in Shetland and the most northerly castle in the British Isles, Muness Castle is a ruinous Z-plan tower house. It dates from the 16th century and consists of a main block with round towers at diagonally opposite corners. The walls are pierced by many gunloops.

The castle was built by Laurence Bruce of Cultmalindie, a Scottish incomer to Shetland. In 1573 he was appointed Chamberlain of the Lordship of Shetland, but his was a corrupt and repressive regime. Ill feeling developed between Bruce and Patrick Stewart, Earl of Orkney, and the Earl landed a force to besiege the castle in 1608, but then withdrew. The castle was burnt in 1627, perhaps by French pirates, although it was later restored. It was abandoned about 1750, and unroofed within 25 years.

Access at all reasonable times.

Tel: 01856 841815

Neidpath Castle

[Map: 155; H5] Off A72, 1 mile W of Peebles, Borders. (NGR: NT 236405 LR: 73)

Nestling on the side of steep gorge overlooking a bend of the River Tweed, Neidpath Castle is an altered L-plan keep with rounded corners and a small courtyard. The keep dates from the 14th century, but was substantially remodelled in the 16th century and later. Turnpike stairs lead to the upper floors, and there is a dark pit prison which is only reached from a hatch in the floor above.

The property belonged to the Frasers, one of whom was Sir Simon Fraser. He was among the Scottish leaders who defeated the English at Roslin in 1302, but was later captured and executed. The castle passed by marriage to the Hays, and was visited by Mary, Queen of Scots in 1563, and then by James VI in 1587. In 1650 it was besieged by Cromwell's forces. The castle held out longer than any other south of the Forth, but was battered into submission, taking damage on the south side. In 1686 it was sold to the Douglas Duke of Queensberry, and later passed to the Earl of Wemyss and March, with whose descendants it remains.

Newark Castle

Neidpath is reputedly haunted by the ghost of a young woman. She fell in love with a local laird, but her father did not think the man good enough for his daughter, and forbade them to marry. The girl pined and died of a broken heart, and her ghost is said to haunt the castle. Manifestations have been reported in recent years.

Gift shop. Museum. Unique batiks depicting Mary Queen of Scots. Tartan collection. WC. Disabled access only to museum and ground floor of castle (up 5 steps). Picnic area. Group concessions. Car and coach parking. £.

Open Easter, then May-beg Sep, Wed-Sat, 10.30-17.00, Sun 12.30-17.00, closed Mon & Tue.
Tel: 01721 720333

Newark Castle

[Map: 156; H6] Off A708, 3 miles W of Selkirk, Borders. (NGR: NT 421294 LR: 73)

Standing in the policies of the mansion of Bowhill, Newark Castle is a substantial ruinous keep and courtyard, which had a gatehouse and wall, sections of which survive.

The property was acquired by Archibald, Earl of Douglas, around 1423. It was kept by the Crown after the downfall of the Black Douglases, and given to Margaret of Denmark, wife of James III, in 1473. The castle was besieged by the English in 1547, and burnt the following year. In 1645 one hundred followers of the Marquis of Montrose, captured after the Battle of Philiphaugh, were shot in the barmkin of Newark. Other prisoners, mostly women (many of them pregnant) and children, were taken to the market place in Selkirk, and there later also shot. It is said that ghostly cries and screams of anguish can sometimes by heard here. The castle was altered for Anna, Duchess of Monmouth and Buccleuch, and Sir Walter Scott visited the castle in 1831 with William and Dorothy Wordsworth.

See Bowhill.

Park open Easter-end Aug; house open Jun, Thu & Sun, 13.00-16.00; Jul, daily 13.00-17.00; Aug, Tue & Thu 13.00-16.00; tel to confirm; other times by appt for educational groups.
Tel: 01750 22204   Web: www.heritageontheweb.co.uk

Newark Castle (HS)

[Map: 157; H4] On A8, 3 miles E of Greenock, Newark, Port Glasgow, Renfrewshire.
(NGR: NS 331745 LR: 63)

Standing on a spit of land into the River Clyde, Newark Castle is a solid and impressive castle. It consists of an extended square keep, dating from the 15th century, to which was later added a gatehouse block and a large range, to form three sides of a courtyard. The remaining side was formerly completed by a wall.

Newark was originally a property of Danielstouns, but passed by marriage to the Maxwells of Calderwood in 1402, who built the castle. James IV was a frequent visitor. One of the family, Patrick Maxwell, was involved in the murders of Patrick Maxwell of Stanely and the Montgomery Earl of Eglinton, in 1584 and 1596 respectively, during a series of feuds. He was married for some 44 years and had 16 children, although he is said to have beaten his wife. The castle was abandoned as a residence early in the 18th century.

Exhibition. Sales area. WC. Car and coach parking. Group concessions. £.
Open Apr-Sep, daily 9.30-18.30; last entry 30 mins before closing.
Tel: 01475 741858

Newhailes (NTS)

[Map: 158; H6] On A6095, 4.5 miles E of Edinburgh, Newhailes Road, Musselburgh, East Lothian.
(NGR: NT 267725 LR: 66)

Lying in acres of fine park and woodland with excellent views over the Forth, Newhailes is a plain but atmospheric symmetrical mansion, built in 1686 by the architect James Smith. There are fine rococo interiors, including the library, and there is a good collection of paintings and portraits.

The property was long known as Whitehill, but the name was changed to Newhailes when the property was purchased by Sir David Dalrymple, calling it after his East Lothian estate of Hailes. It was extended about 1750. Newhailes was visited by many leading figures of the Scottish Enlightenment.

One-hour guided tours of house from 13.00 - booking essential. Visitor centre. Plant centre. Parking. ££.
House and visitor centre open Easter, then May-Sep, Thu-Mon 12.00-17.00; estate open all year, daily 10.00-18.00.
Tel: 0131 665 1546

Newliston

[Map: 159; H5] Off B800, 8 miles W of Edinburgh, Kirkliston, West Lothian..
(NGR: NT 110736 LR: 66)

Newliston, a tall classical mansion, was built in 1789 by the architect Robert Adam for the Hogg family, who purchased the lands in the mid 18th century. An older house on the site, dating from the 17th century, was the home of John Dalrymple, 2nd Earl of Stair, who died in 1747.

The gardens and park, which feature rhododendrons, azaleas and water features, were laid out at this time. The stable block dates from 1723, and may have been designed by William Adam, and there are costumes on display.

Tearoom. Ride-on steam model railway Sun only (14.00-17.00). Disabled access to grounds. Parking. £.
Open May-4 Jun, Wed-Sun 14.00-18.00; other times by appt.
Tel: 0131 333 3231

Noltland Castle (HS)

[Map: 160; A6] Off B9066, NE side of island of Westray, Orkney. (NGR: HY 430487 LR: 5)

A strong and grim stronghold somewhat out of place on the peaceful Orkney island of Westray, Noltland Castle is a large ruined Z-plan tower house. The present stronghold was built in the 16th century, and a later courtyard survives with the remains of an L-plan range of buildings. The tower has many gunloops

An earlier castle here was built by Thomas Tulloch, Bishop of Orkney, in 1420, and towards the end of the 15th century was besieged by the Sinclairs of Warsetter. The present castle was built by Gilbert Balfour, Master of the Household to Mary, Queen of Scots. He had been involved in the murders of Cardinal Beaton in 1546, for which he was imprisoned, and Lord Darnley in 1567. He supported Mary after she fled to England, but left Scotland, and served in the Swedish army until his death by execution in 1576 after plotting against the Swedish king.

The castle was seized in 1592 by Patrick Stewart, Earl of Orkney, in order to get payment of a debt. Some of the Marquis of Montrose's men took refuge here after their defeat at Carbisdale in 1650, and the castle was later held by Cromwell's men. Noltland was abandoned about 1760.

A death in the Balfour family was reputedly heralded by a ghostly howling dog, the 'Boky Hound', while births and marriages were announced by eerie spectral lights. The castle is also said to have had a brownie.

Orkney ferries from Kirkwall (01856 872044).

Open mid Jun-Sep, daily 9.30-18.30; last ticket sold 30 mins before closing.

Tel: 01856 841815

Old Gala House

[Map: 161; H6] Off A7, Scott Crescent, Galashiels, Borders.
(NGR: NT 492357 LR: 73)

Old Gala, a rambling mansion, incorporates an altered 16th-century tower house at one end, and an extended T-plan building of 1611 in the middle. There is a painted ceiling, dating from 1635; as well as a garden.

It may stand on the site of a 15th-century castle of the Douglases, which was destroyed in 1544. The property passed by marriage from the Pringles of Gala to the Scotts in 1632. The building is now used as a community and art centre, and there is a museum with displays about the occupants of the house and Galashiels.

Explanatory displays. Gift shop. Tearoom. Garden. Disabled access to ground floor. Audio guide available. Tour groups. Parking.

Open Apr-May and Aug-Oct, Tue-Sat 10.00-16.00; Jun-Jul, Mon-Sat 10.00-16.00, Sun 13.00-16.00.

Tel: 01896 752611   Web: www.scotborders.gov.uk/outabout/museums

Orchardton Tower (HS)

[Map: 162; J5] Off A711, 4 miles S of Dalbeattie, Dumfries and Galloway.
(NGR: NX 817551 LR: 84)

Unique in Scotland as the only free-standing round tower house, Orchardton dates from the 15th and 16th centuries and rises to four storeys with a corbelled-out parapet. Foundations of courtyard buildings survive.

The lands of Orchardton passed to the Cairnses early in the 15th century, and they built the tower, but the property later passed by marriage to the Maxwells. During the Jacobite Rising of 1745, one of the family, Sir Robert Maxwell, was wounded and then captured at Culloden in 1746. He was taken to Carlisle for trial and execution. He tried to destroy his personal papers, but was prevented, and his commission as an officer in the French army was found. He was thereafter treated as a prisoner of war, and was exiled to France rather than being executed. He later returned to Orchardton. Sir Walter Scott made use of this story in his novel 'Guy Mannering'. *Car parking.*

Access at all reasonable times.

Orkney Museum, Kirkwall

[Map: 163; A6] Off A964 or A965, Broad Street, Kirkwall, Orkney (NGR: HY 446109 LR: 6)

One of the finest town houses in Scotland, the Orkney Museum is housed in Tankerness House, a 16th-century building with court-yard and gardens. The museum charts the islands' archaeology and history.

The house was built as a deanery for the nearby cathedral, and is dated 1574. It passed to the

Orchardton Tower

Baikies of Tankerness in the 17th century, who were successful merchants in Kirkwall. Arthur Baikie was Provost of the burgh.

Guided tours by arrangement. Explanatory displays. Gift shop. Garden. WC. Disabled access. Parking nearby.

Open all year: Oct-Apr, Mon-Sat 10.30-12.30 & 13.30-17.00; May-Sep, Mon-Sat 10.30-17.00, also Sun 14.00-17.00.

Tel: 01856 873191   Web: www.orkneyheritage.com

Paxton House

[Map: 164; H7] Off B6461, 7 miles S of Eyemouth, Paxton, Borders. (NGR: NT 935530 LR: 74)

In a picturesque setting overlooking the Tweed and into England, Paxton House is a fine classical mansion with a colonnaded central block and two flanking wings, and was built in 1756 for Patrick Home of Billie. The house was erected for his intended bride, Charlotte de Brandt, daughter of King Frederick the Great of Prussia. The house was probably designed by Robert, John and James Adam; and in 1811 a gallery and library were added to designs by Robert Reid. There is access to 12 period rooms, and a fine collection of furniture. Paxton is now an outstation of the National Galleries of Scotland, and houses 70 paintings.

There are 80 acres of garden, woodland and parkland.

Exhibitions of pictures and furniture. Gift shop. Licensed tearoom. Gardens, woodlands and 80 acres of park land. Picnic area. Plant centre. Adventure playground. Partial disabled access to house. Car and coach parking. ££. Function suite for hire.

Open Good Fri-Oct, daily 10.00-17.00, last admission 45 mins before closing; shop and tearoom, 10.00-17.30; grounds 10.00-sunset; open to groups/schools all year by appt.

Tel: 01289 386291   Web: www.paxtonhouse.com

Peel Ring of Lumphanan (HS)

[Map: 165; E6] Off A93, 5 miles NE of Aboyne, Lumphanan, Kincardine & Deeside.
(NGR: NJ 576037 LR: 37)

Peel Ring of Lumphanan is a large but low motte with a wide ditch, and dates from the 12th century. It was formerly enclosed by a strong stone wall, and Halton House, a 15th-century block, was built on the motte and occupied until 1782. Nothing remains of this building except foundations.

The property was held by the Durwards in the 13th century, and visited by Edward I of England in 1296. It has passed to the Halketts by 1370, and then the Irvines in the 15th century. Macbeth is believed to have been slain at Lumphanan in 1057, and there are several sites associated with him. *Parking.*

Access at all reasonable times.

Tel: 01667 460232

Pitmedden House and Garden (NTS)

[Map: 166; D6] On A920, 8 miles NE of Inverurie, Pitmedden, Aberdeenshire.
(NGR: NJ 885281 LR: 38)

Pitmedden House is a 17th-century house, remodelled in 1853 and in 1954, and may incorporate part of an older building. It stands on the site of a castle.

The castle was a property of the Setons. Alexander Seton of Pitmedden was a Royalist and was slain when he was shot through the heart at Dee Bridge in 1639 while carrying the king's standard.

The property passed to the Bannermans in the 17th century, then to the Keiths.

The house has an extensive 17th-century five-acre walled garden, which is open to the public, and features sundials, pavilions and fountains dotted among formal flower beds. There is also the Museum of Farming Life and visitor centre, as well as a wildlife garden and woodland walk.

Museum of Farming Life. Gift shop. Tea room. WC. Disabled facilities and access. Woodland walk and wildlife garden. Car and coach parking. ££.

House not open; garden, museum and visitor centre open May-Sep, daily 10.00-17.30; last entry 30 mins before closing; grounds open all year, daily.

Tel: 01651 842352

Pittencrieff House

[Map: 167; H5] Off A994, Pittencrieff Park, Dunfermline, Fife. (NGR: NT 087873 LR: 65)

Built with stone from the nearby royal palace at Dunfermline, Pittencrieff House is a 17th-century T-plan house of three storeys and a garret. The walls are harled and yellow-washed, and it stands in a public park.

Pittencrieff was a property of Dunfermline Abbey, but passed to the Setons after the Reformation, then several other families. The house was remodelled, to form three galleries, by Sir Robert Lorimer in 1908 when it was bought by Andrew Carnegie. He gave the property to the people of Dunfermline, and the house now has a collection of costumes and displays on the history of the house and park, as well as an art gallery. The park is laid out over 76 acres and there are glasshouses, aviary, animals and an art deco pavilion with restaurants.

Audio-visual presentation. Explanatory displays. Gift shop. Picnic area in park. Gardens. WC in park. Disabled access to ground floor. Parking in park.

Open all year: May-Sep 11.00-17.00; Oct-Apr 11.00-16.00; closed Christmas and New Year.

Tel: 01383 722935/313838   Web: www.fifeattractions.com

Pollok House (NTS)

[Map: 168; H4] Off B768, Pollok Country Park, Pollokshaws area of Glasgow. (NGR: NS 549619 LR: 64)

Pollok House is a large mansion, first built about 1750 and then remodelled and extended by the architect Sir Robert Rowand Anderson in 1890. Among its many attractions are the suite of servants' quarters, showing life for those below stairs in the 1900s. There was a castle, with a ditch and draw-bridge, a vestige of which remains with a garden wall, close to the stable yard.

It was a property of the Maxwells from the mid 13th century. Pollok was gifted to the City of Glasgow in 1966, and the fascinating Burrell Collection is situated within the grounds. The house is used to display the Stirling Maxwell collection of Spanish and European paintings, furniture, ceramics and silver. The house stands in a country park with fine formal and walled gardens, woodland and parkland.

Guided tours. Gift shop. Licensed restaurant. WC. Partial disabled access. Parking. ££.

Open all year, daily 10.00-17.00; closed 25-26 Dec and 1-2 Jan.

Tel: 0141 616 6410

Preston Tower (NTS)

[Map: 169; H6] Off A198, SE of Prestonpans, Preston, East Lothian. (NGR: NT 393742 LR: 66)

Preston Tower is a strong but ruinous L-plan keep of four storeys, possibly incorporating work from as early as the 14th century, although it is substantially older. Two further storeys were added above the parapet in the 17th century. It stands in attractive gardens with a laburnum arch, clipped yew hedges and a herb garden.

Preston had several owners before passing by marriage to the Hamiltons at the end of

the 14th century. It was torched in 1544 by the Earl of Hertford, and again in 1650 by Cromwell. After being restored, it was accidentally burnt out again in 1663, then abandoned for nearby Preston House. One of the family was Robert Hamilton, who was a noted Covenanter and prominent in the battles of Drumclog and Bothwell Brig. The family were forfeited in 1684, but recovered the property in the 19th century. The tower was consolidated in 1936, purchased by The National Trust for Scotland in 1969, and is under the guardianship of the local council. The building is said to be haunted by a 'Green Lady'.

Garden. Parking nearby.

Gardens open all year, daily dawn to dusk – the tower may be viewed from the exterior.

Tel: 01875 810232

Provost Skene's House, Aberdeen

[Map: 170; E7] Off A92, 45 Guest Row, off Broad Street, Aberdeen. (NGR: NJ 943064 LR: 38)

Provost Skene's House is a fine 16th-century fortified town house. A magnificent 17th-century plaster ceiling and wood panelling survives, and the painted gallery features a unique cycle of tempera wall and ceiling painting depicting Christ's life.

The house was a property of George Skene of Rubislaw, a wealthy merchant, from 1669. The Duke of Cumberland stayed here for six weeks in 1746 on his way to Culloden and the defeat of the Jacobites. Other rooms include a suite of Georgian chambers, and an Edwardian nursery, and there is also a museum of local history and social life.

Period room settings. 17th-century ceiling and wall paintings, costume gallery, and local history exhibitions. Sales area. Coffee shop. WC. Public parking nearby.

Open all year, Mon-Sat 10.00-17.00, Sun 13.00-16.30; last entry 30 mins before closing; closed 25/26/31 Dec and 1/2 Jan.

Tel: 01224 641086   Web: www.aagm.co.uk

Rammerscales House

[Map: 171; I5] On B9020, 3 miles SW of Lockerbie, Dumfries and Galloway.
(NGR: NY 081777 LR: 85)

Standing on a high slope of the Torthorwald Hills, Rammerscales is a fine 18th-century mansion of four storeys, with magnificent views over Annandale. In Adam style and mostly unaltered, the mansion was home to the Mounsey family in the 18th century, but is now a property of the Bell Macdonalds. It houses rare contemporary art, and there are attractive grounds with walled gardens.

Guided tours for parties. Car and coach parking. £££.

Last week in Jul; 1st three weeks in Aug: Sun-Fri 14.00-17.00, closed Sat.

Tel: 01387 810229   Web: www.rammerscales.co.uk

Ravenscraig Castle (HS)

[Map: 172; G5] Off A955, 1 mile NE of Kirkcaldy, Ravenscraig, Fife. (NGR: NT 291925 LR: 59)

On the coast above the Firth of Forth, Ravenscraig Castle is a ruinous castle and courtyard, dating from the 15th century but altered in later centuries. It was designed as one of the first castles in Scotland to withstand and return artillery fire. It consists of two D-plan towers, with very thick walls, and a courtyard cut off from the mainland by a deep ditch. The towers were linked by a two-storey block with a broad parapet. Only part of the building is now accessible.

James II, who died when a cannon exploded during the siege of Roxburgh Castle, started to build Ravenscraig before 1460 for Mary of Gueldres. She died at the castle three years later. It was forced upon William Sinclair, then Earl of Orkney, by James III in return for the Earldom and Kirkwall Castle, on Orkney, which the King wanted for himself. The Sinclairs held the property until 1898.

Parking.

Access at all reasonable times – some of the building cannot be entered.

Red Castle

[Map: 173; G6] Off A92, 5 miles S of Montrose, Lunan, Angus. (NGR: NO 687510 LR: 54)

Red Castle is a striking and impressive ruin in a prominent location above the Lunan Water. The castle dates from the 12th-century, although the keep, one half of which survives, was added in the 14th or 15th century.

The original castle was built by the Barclays, and was used by William the Lyon for hunting. Robert the Bruce gave the castle to Hugh, 6th Earl of Ross, in 1328, and it later passed to the Stewart Lord Innermeath. It was attacked by Protestants led by James Gray in 1579, 1580 and then 1581. It was last occupied by the Episcopal minister, James Rait, and the property later passed to the Guthries. *Parking nearby.*

Access at all reasonable times – the castle may be in a dangerous condition and care should be taken.

Rothesay Castle (HS)

[Map: 174; H4] Off A845, Rothesay, Bute. (NGR: NS 086646 LR: 63)

Surrounded by a water-filled moat and built on a mound or motte, Rothesay Castle has a substantial shell keep of the 12th century, with four later round towers. In the late 15th century a large rectangular keep and gatehouse were added, which was completed by James V after 1541. The sea used to be closer to the castle.

The castle was attacked and taken by Norsemen in the 1230s, who cut a hole in the wall with their axes. It was captured in 1263 by King Hakon of Norway, before he was defeated at the Battle of Largs. The Stewarts were keepers of the castle. Rothesay was held by the English during the Wars of Independence, but was taken by Robert the Bruce, only to be captured again by the English under Edward Balliol in 1334, once again to be retaken by the Scots.

It was a favourite residence of Robert II and Robert III, who may have died here rather than at Dundonald in 1406. Five years earlier Robert III made David his son Duke of Rothesay, a title since taken by the eldest son of the kings of Scots and currently held by Prince Charles (David, himself, did not fare well and was starved to death at Falkland). The castle was besieged by the Earl of Ross in 1462, the Master of Ruthven in 1527, and in 1544 was captured by the Earl of Lennox on behalf of the English. James V had visited in 1530, and completed the gatehouse block after 1541. In the 1650s the castle was held for Charles I, but was later taken by Cromwell, whose men damaged the building. Argyll's forces torched the place in 1685. Restoration was undertaken in 1812 and in the 1870s.

Ruthven Barracks

One story has the castle haunted by a Lady Isobel, seen on the 'Bloody Stair'. She killed herself after her family were slain by Norsemen and one of them desired her as his wife (or perhaps just desired her).

Explanatory displays and panels. Audio-visual display. Kiosk. WC. Car parking nearby. Group concessions. £.

Open all year: Apr-Sep, daily 9.30-18.30; Oct-Mar, Sat-Wed 9.30-16.30, closed Thu & Fri; last ticket sold 30 mins before closing; closed 25/26 Dec and 1/2 Jan.

Tel: 01700 502691

Ruthven Barracks (HS)

[Map: 175; E5] Off A9, 1 mile S of Kingussie, Ruthven Barracks, Highland. (NGR: NN 764997 LR: 35)
The ruinous remains of a large barracks stands on the substantial earthworks of a 13th-century castle. The castle was held by the Comyns, but passed to Alexander Stewart, the Wolf of Badenoch, as the chief stronghold of his lordship. In 1451 it passed to the Gordon, Earl of Huntly, but in that year was sacked by John MacDonald, Earl of Ross. It was rebuilt by 1459 when James II visited. Mary, Queen of Scots stayed at the castle. It was twice damaged by fire, and in 1689 was attacked by Jacobites. In 1718 the castle was demolished and replaced by the barracks for Hanoverian troops. This was held by government forces in 1746, but was eventually taken and burnt by Jacobite forces. It was not restored.

One story has the ghosts of the Wolf of Badenoch and his men haunting the site. It is said that they were damned after he challenged the Devil to a game of chess.

Car parking.

Access at all reasonable times.

Tel: 01667 460232

Sanquhar Castle

[Map: 176; I5] Off A76, 0.25 miles S of Sanquhar, Dumfries and Galloway.
(NGR: NS 786092 LR: 78)
Sanquhar Castle is a ruined castle, dating from the 13th century but with later work, and consists of the remains of an altered keep and ranges of buildings around a courtyard. A four-storey tower stands at one corner.

The lands passed by marriage to the Crichtons in the 14th century. James VI visited the castle in 1617. The family were made Earls of Dumfries in 1633, but six years later sold the property to Sir William Douglas of Drumlanrig, who was later made Duke of Queensberry. The family moved to Drumlanrig Castle, and Sanquhar was abandoned to become ruined.

Two ghosts reputedly haunt the castle. One is the 'White Lady', said to be the spirit of a young golden-haired woman, Marion of Dalpeddar, who is said to have disappeared in 1590. A skeleton of a girl was reportedly found during excavations in 1875-6. Another ghost is said to be that of a man wrongly hanged by one of the Crichtons.

Open all year: ruins are in a poor state of repair and great care should be taken.

Scalloway Castle (HS)

[Map: 177; C7] Off A970, Scalloway, Shetland. (NGR: HU 404392 LR: 4)
Located on a peninsula into East Voe, Scalloway Castle is an impressive and elegant L-plan tower house, dating from the 17th century, but ruinous although complete to the wallhead. There is a main block of four storeys and an attic, and a smaller square offset wing. Turrets crown the building and the walls are pierced by shot-holes.

The castle was built by Patrick Stewart, Earl of Orkney, in 1600. He was unpopular with both the

Orcadians and the folk of Shetland, forcing local people to work on the castle and taxing them to pay for materials. Earl Patrick was executed in 1615. The castle was occupied by Cromwell's forces in the 1650s, and abandoned by the end of the 17th century.

Explanatory displays. Car parking.

Open Mon-Sat 9.30-17.00 (or as Shetland Woollen Company shop). Sun, key available from the Royal Hotel.

Tel: 01856 841815

Scone Palace

[Map: 178; G5] Off A93, 2 miles N of Perth, Scone, Perthshire. (NGR: NO 114267 LR: 58)

In acres of wild gardens and parkland, Scone (pronounced 'Skoon') Palace is a substantial castellated mansion, dating from 1802 and designed by William Atkinson. It incorporates part of the palace built by the Ruthvens in the 1580s, itself probably created out of the Abbot's Lodging.

The Kings of Scots were inaugurated at the Moot Hill, near the present palace, from the reign of Kenneth MacAlpin. An abbey was founded here in the 12th century, although there are no remains; and The Stone of Destiny, also called the Stone of Scone, was kept here, until taken to Westminster Abbey by Edward I in 1296. It was returned to Edinburgh Castle in 1996. The last king to be inaugurated here was Charles I in 1651.

The property was owned by the Ruthvens in 1580, although it passed to the Murrays after the Gowrie Conspiracy in 1600: David Murray of Gospertie had been one of those to save James VI's life.

The family were made Viscounts Stormont in 1602, and Earls of Mansfield in 1776. James VIII and III held 'court' here in 1716, and Bonnie Prince Charlie visited in 1745.

Fine collections of furniture, clocks, needlework and porcelain. Gift shops. Restaurant. Tearoom. WC. Picnic area. 100 acres of wild gardens. Maze. Adventure playground. Meetings and conferences. Disabled access to state rooms & restaurant. Car and coach parking. Group concessions. £££.

Open Apr-Oct, daily 9.30-17.30; last entry 30 mins before closing; grounds close at 18.00; other times by appt.

Tel: 01738 552300   Web: www.scone-palace.co.uk

Scotstarvit Tower (HS)

[Map: 179; G6] Off A916, 2 miles S of Cupar, Hill of Tarvit, Fife. (NGR: NO 370113 LR: 59)

A fine and imposing building, Scotstarvit Tower is a tall L-plan tower house of six storeys and a garret. It dates from the 15th and 16th centuries, and was originally a property of the Inglis family. It was sold to the Scotts in 1611, one of whom, Sir John Scott of Scotstarvit, was an eminent historian. The property was sold to the Gourlays about 1780, then to the Wemyss family, then to the Sharps in 1904.

Also see Hill of Tarvit.

Owned by NTS; administered by Historic Scotland. Key available at Hill of Tarvit, which is open Easter, then May to September.

Tel: 01334 653127

Shambellie House

[Map: 180; I5] Off A710, 7 miles S of Dumfries, Shambellie, New Abbey, Dumfries and Galloway. (NGR: NX 960665 LR: 84)

Set in mature woodlands, Shambellie House dates from the 19th century and was designed by the architect David Bryce for the Stewart family, who had held the property from the 17th century or earlier. The house is home to the National Museum of Costume, and each year there are new exhibits of European fashionable dress from the National Costume Collection.

Guided tours. Explanatory displays. Gift shop. Tearoom. WC. Picnic area. Gardens. Disabled access to gardens. Limited parking. £. Season ticket available for all National Museums of Scotland sites (£££).

Open Apr-Oct, daily 10.00-17.00.

Tel: 01387 850375   Web: www.nms.ac.uk/costume

Skaill House

[Map: 181; A5] Off B9056, 6 miles N of Stromness, Skaill, Breckness, Orkney. (NGR: HY 234186 LR: 6)

Standing close by the important and hugely impressive Neolithic village of Skara Brae, Skaill House is the most complete 17th-century mansion house in Orkney. The oldest part is a two-storey block and courtyard, which was extended over the following centuries into a large complex of buildings. It was built for Bishop George Graham in the 1620s. Captain Cook's dinner service from *The Discovery* is kept at the house, and the building is surrounded by extensive gardens.

The building is reputedly haunted. Manifestations have included the sound of feet from unoccupied areas, and the apparition of an old woman.

Guided tours. Explanatory displays. Gift shop. WC. Disabled access. Garden. Car and coach parking. Group concessions. ££. Joint entry ticket for all Orkney monuments (£££).

Skaill House open Apr-Sep, daily 9.30-18.30; last entry 30 mins before closing.

Tel: 01856 841501   Web: www.skaillhouse.com

Skipness Castle (HS)

[Map: 182; H3] Off B8001, 7 miles S of Tarbert, Skipness, Argyll. (NGR: NR 907577 LR: 62)

In a peaceful location with fine views across to Arran, Skipness Castle is a ruinous 13th-century courtyard castle, which is enclosed by a curtain wall with three ruinous towers. There is a well-preserved tower house of four storeys and an attic with an external stone stair to the first floor. The main entrance to the courtyard was from the sea, which was defended by a gatetower with a portcullis and machiolation.

The first castle was probably built by the MacSweens around 1247, and it was strengthened against the Norsemen later that century. It was held by the MacDonald Lords of the Isles until 1493 when

they were forfeited. The castle was then granted to the Forresters, but was soon acquired by the Campbells. It was besieged unsuccessfully by Alaisdair Colkitto MacDonald in the 1640s, but was abandoned at the end of the 17th century to be used as a farm. Skipness House was built nearby, and either this building or the castle is said to have had a 'Green Lady'.

The ruins of a 13th-century chapel, Kilbrannan, dedicated to St Brendan, lie to the south-east of the castle. There are fine graveslabs.

Explanatory boards. Car parking near castle.

Access at all reasonable times: short walk to castle, then walk to chapel which may be muddy.

Smailholm Tower (HS)

[Map: 183; H6] Off B6397, 6 miles W of Kelso, Smailholm, Borders. (NGR: NT 637346 LR: 74)

Standing on a rocky outcrop in a windswept spot, Smailholm Tower is a strong and plain 15th-century tower house, rectangular in plan. It stood in a small walled courtyard enclosing ranges of buildings, although these are very ruinous. The basement is vaulted as is the top storey, and there are wall walks on two sides of the tower.

It was a property of the Pringle family from 1408. David Pringle of Smailholm was killed, together with his four sons, at the Battle of Flodden in 1513. The tower was attacked by the English in 1543, and again three years later, when the garrison of Wark made off with 60 cattle and

four prisoners. The property was sold to the Scotts of Harden in 1645, but the tower was abandoned about 1700. Sir Walter Scott came here as a boy – as his grandfather held nearby Sandyknowe. The tower houses an exhibition of dolls illustrating some of the Border ballads from Scott's *Minstrelsy of the Scottish Borders.*

Explanatory displays. Sales area. Car and coach parking. £.

Open Apr-Sep, daily 9.30-18.30; Oct, Sat-Wed 9.30-16.30, closed Thu-Fri; Nov-Mar wknds only 9.30-16.30; last ticket 30 mins before closing; closed 25/26 Dec and 1/2 Jan.

Tel: 01573 460365

Sorbie Castle

[Map: 184; J4] Off B7052, 2 miles W of Garlieston, E of Sorbie, Dumfries and Galloway. (NGR: NX 451471 LR: 83)

Once a strong but comfortable fortress, Sorbie Castle is a ruinous L-plan tower house of three storeys and an attic, which dates from the 16th century.

The lands belonged to Whithorn Abbey, but passed to the Hannays by 1529, or earlier, who built the castle. The family had a bitter feud with the Murrays of Broughton. In 1640 John Hannay was killed in a quarrel, the family was ruined, and the property was sold to the Stewarts of Garlies, Earls of Galloway, within 30 years. The castle was inhabited until 1748. The remains have been consolidated for visitors by members of the Hannay clan.

Open all year.

Sorn Castle

[Map: 185; I4] Off B743, 3 miles E of Mauchline, Ayrshire. (NGR: NS 548269 LR: 70)

Standing on a height in beautiful grounds above the River Ayr, Sorn Castle is an altered and extended keep of three storeys and an attic, which dates from the 14th century. The old tower was extended down the centuries, including restoration in 1865 by the architect David Bryce.

The lands belonged to the Keiths of Galston, but passed by marriage to the Hamiltons of Cadzow in 1406, then to the Setons of Winton. James VI visited the castle, and it was garrisoned against Covenanters in the reign of Charles II. It was sold to the Campbell Earl of Loudoun about 1680, then to the Somervilles at the end of the 18th century, and finally to the McIntyre family in 1900, who still occupy the house.

Historic castle set in beautiful grounds on the River Ayr.

Guided tours: 2nd 2 weeks of Jul and 1st 2 weeks of Aug.

Tel: 01290 551555

Spynie Palace (HS)

[Map: 186; D5] Off A941, 2.5 miles N of Elgin, Spynie, Moray. (NGR: NJ 231658 LR: 28)

Although called a palace (as it was the residence of the Bishops of Moray), in reality Spynie Palace this is one of the most impressive castles in Scotland. It consists of a massive 15th-century keep, Davy's Tower, at one corner of a large courtyard enclosed by a wall and with square corner towers. In one wall is a gatehouse, and there were ranges of buildings, including a chapel, within the courtyard walls. The keep is now a shell and many of the buildings are quite ruinous.

In 1200 Bishop Richard moved the cathedral of Moray to Spynie, where it stayed for 24 years before going to Elgin, now with its grand ruinous cathedral. Later bishops fortified a promontory in Spynie Loch, once a sea loch with its own port.

The palace was probably built by Bishop Innes, after Elgin Cathedral had been burnt by Alexander Stewart, the Wolf of Badenoch. Bishop David Stewart, who died in 1475, excommunicated the Gordon Earl of Huntly, and built the great keep, Davy's Tower, to defend himself against Huntly. James IV visited the palace in 1493 and 1505, as did Mary, Queen of Scots, in 1562, and then later the

4th Earl of Bothwell, her third husband, after fleeing from the debacle at Carberry. He eventually went to Orkney and the Continent

After the Reformation the palace was used by Protestant bishops. James VI stayed here in 1589. General Munro besieged the palace in 1640, and compelled Bishop Guthrie to surrender it, and then Guthrie was imprisoned. The last resident bishop was Colin Falconer, who died here in 1686. The building then became ruinous.

Explanatory panels. Gift shop. WC. Picnic area. Car and coach parking. £. Joint ticket with Elgin Cathedral available (£).

Open Apr-Sep, daily 9.30-18.30; Oct-Mar, wknds only 9.30-16.30; last ticket sold 30 mins before closing; closed 25/25 Dec and 1/2 Jan.

Tel: 01343 546358

St Andrews Castle (HS)

[Map: 187; G6] Off A91, St Andrews, Fife. (NGR: NO 513169 LR: 59)

Standing close to remains of the splendid but very fragmentary cathedral, St Andrews Castle is a ruined courtyard castle, enclosed by a wall. There was a gatehouse and towers at the corners, one of which contains a bottle dungeon cut into the rock. Much of the castle is very ruined. It stands in a fine location by the sea in the attractive burgh of St Andrews.

It was held by the bishops of St Andrews, and the first castle here was built by Bishop Roger, but was dismantled by Robert the Bruce around 1310. It was rebuilt in 1336 by the English in support of Edward Balliol, but was captured by Sir Andrew Moray the following year, and slighted again. At the end of the 14th century, Bishop Trail rebuilt the castle.

Stirling Castle

Cardinal David Beaton strengthened the castle by adding two round blockhouses, now destroyed. In 1546 a band of Protestants murdered Beaton in the castle, and hung his naked body from one of the tower. Reinforced by others, including John Knox, they held the castle for a year. The besiegers tunnelled towards the walls, and the defenders countermined and captured their tunnel. Both tunnels still survive. It was only with the arrival of a French fleet that the garrison surrendered and became galley slaves, John Knox among them.

The castle was restored to the new Protestant bishops in 1612. However, the castle had lost importance, and by 1654 the town council had stone removed from the castle to repair the harbour.

Visitor centre with fine exhibition. Explanatory panels. Gift shop. WC. Disabled access and WC. Car parking nearby. Group concessions. £. Combined ticket for cathedral & castle is available (££).

Open all year: Apr-Sep, daily 9.30-18.30; Oct-Mar, daily 9.30-16.30; last ticket sold 30 mins before closing; closed 25/26 Dec and 1/2 Jan.

Tel: 01334 477196

Stirling Castle (HS)

[Map: 188; H5] Off A872, Upper Castle Hill, in Stirling. (NGR: NS 790940 LR: 57)

One of the most important and powerful castles in Scotland, Stirling Castle stands on a high rock, and consists of a courtyard castle, which dates in part from the 12th century. The castle is entered through the 18th-century outer defences and 16th-century forework of which the Prince's Tower and the gatehouse survive, but the Elphinstone Tower has been reduced to its base. The gatehouse leads to the Lower Square, which is bordered on one side by the King's Old Building, and on another by the gable of the Great Hall.

A road leads between the King's Old Buildings and the hall to the Upper Square. The Chapel Royal is built on one side of the square, as is the Great Hall, which was completed during the reign of James IV. The Chapel Royal was remodelled by James VI in 1594, and James was (earlier!) baptised here. The ceiling and part of the walls were decorated in 1628. By the early 20th century, the building was used as a school and dining room. The Hall has five fireplaces, and had a magnificent hammer-beam ceiling – which had not survived, but has been replaced.

Other features of interest are the kitchens, the wall walk and the nearby 'King's Knot', the earthworks of a magnificent ornamental garden, which once had a pleasure canal. It was probably laid out in 1628 for Charles I.

The earliest recorded castle at Stirling was used by Malcolm Canmore in the 11th century. Alexander I died here in 1124, as did William the Lyon in 1214. Edward I of England captured the castle in 1304 when he used – although after the garrison had surrendered – a siege engine called the 'War Wolf'. William Wallace took the castle for the Scots, but it was retaken by the English who held it until the Battle of Bannockburn in 1314.

Robert the Bruce had the castle slighted, but it was rebuilt by Edward III of England, after his victory of Halidon Hill in 1333, in support of Edward Balliol. The English garrison was besieged in 1337 by Andrew Moray, but it was not until 1342 that the Scots recovered the castle.

James II was born here in 1430, as was James III in 1451. James II lured the 8th Earl of Douglas to it in 1452, murdered him, and had his body tossed out of one of the windows, despite promising safe conduct. Mary, Queen of Scots, was crowned in the old chapel in 1543, and the future James VI was baptised here in 1566. James VI stayed here in 1617, as did Charles I in 1633, and Charles II in 1650. In 1651 the castle was besieged by Monck for Cromwell, but it surrendered after a few days because of a mutiny in the garrison.

It was in a poor state of repair in the 18th century, but the garrison harried the Jacobites during both the 1715 and 1745 Risings, and the Jacobites besieged the castle after the Battle of Falkirk in 1746, although not very successfully. After 1745, the castle was subdivided to be used as a barracks. In 1964 the army left. There is also the Museum of the Argyll and Sutherland Highlanders, telling the story of the regiment from 1794 to the present day, and featuring uniforms, silver, paintings, colours, pipe banners and commentaries.

Some of the fine 16th-century town wall also survives.

Guided tours are available and can be booked in advance. Exhibition of life in the royal palace, introductory display, medieval kitchen display. Museum of the Argyll and Sutherland Highlanders. Gift shop. Restaurant. WC. Disabled access and WC. Car and coach parking. Group concessions. £££

Open all year: Apr-Sep daily 9.30-16.00; Oct-Mar daily 9.30-17.00; last ticket sold 45 mins before closing – joint ticket with Argyll's Lodging; closed 25/26 Dec; open 1/2 Jan: tel for opening times.
Tel: 01786 450000

Stobhall

[Map: 189; G5] On A93, 7 miles N of Perth, Stobhall, Perthshire. (NGR: NO 132344 LR: 53)
Set in a picturesque spot, Stobhall is a 16th-century castle, consisting of ranges of buildings, one a tower house, within a courtyard. There is also a chapel with a tempera painted ceiling. The castle may stand on the site of an older stronghold, perhaps dating from as early as the 12th century.

Stobhall was held by the Muschetts, but passed by marriage to the Drummonds in 1360. It was their stronghold until 1487, when they moved to Drummond Castle. The property was forfeited for the family's part in 1745 Jacobite Rising. It passed to the Willoughbys, before returning to the Drummonds, and is now the home of the present Earl of Perth.

WC. Partial disabled access to chapel and Rose Garden and WC. Limited parking. ££
Gardens and chapel open 7-22 May & 30 Jul-7 Aug, daily 14.00-17.30; tours to Dowerhouse staircase, drawing room and folly 14.30 and 16.30; castle not open.
Tel: 01821 640332   Web: www.stobhall.com

Strathaven Castle

[Map: 190; H5] On A71, Strathaven, Lanarkshire. (NGR: NS 703445 LR: 71)

On a rocky mound above the village, Strathaven Castle is a ruinous castle, which consists of the remains of a square range and round tower. There was a castle here from the 15th century or earlier.

The property was held by the Bairds, then the Sinclairs, then the Douglases. The castle was surrendered to James II in 1455, and sacked and probably destroyed following the fall of the Black Douglases. It then passed to the Stewart Lord Avondale in 1457, who built, or rebuilt, the castle. In the 16th century it was acquired by Sir James Hamilton of Finnart, and occupied by the Hamiltons until 1717, after which it was abandoned and fell into ruin. The building has been consolidated. A skeleton, sealed up in one of the walls, is said to have been found when part of the castle was demolished. *Explanatory board. Parking nearby.*

Access at all reasonable times.

Tantallon Castle (HS)

[Map: 191; H6] Off A198, 3 miles E of North Berwick, Tantallon, East Lothian.
(NGR: NT 596851 LR: 67)

Located in a strong position on high cliffs above the sea, Tantallon Castle is a large and strong courtyard castle, dating from the 14th century but now ruinous. It probably presents the most impressive edifice of any castle in Scotland; and consists of a massively thick 80-foot-high curtain wall, blocking off a promontory. In front of the wall is a deep ditch, and at each end are ruined towers: one round, and one D-shaped. The shell of a massive keep-gatehouse stands at the middle of the wall, and rises to six storeys. Within the castle walls are the remains of a range of buildings.

The castle was built by William Douglas, 1st Earl of Douglas, about 1350. William waylaid and slew his godfather, another William, the infamous 'Knight of Liddlesdale', and secured his position as the most powerful lord in the Borders. George Douglas, his son, became the first Earl of Angus, the 'Red Douglases'.

Archibald, 5th Earl, known as 'Bell-the-Cat', hanged James III's favourites from the bridge at Lauder. He entered into a treasonable pact with Henry VII of England, which led to James IV besieging Tantallon. In 1513 Douglas died, and his two sons were then killed at the Battle of Flodden. The castle was attacked in 1528, although unsuccessfully, by James V; and Mary, Queen of Scots, visited in 1566. In 1651 Cromwell sent an army to attack the castle, as men from Tantallon, as well as

Dirleton, had been attacking his lines of communication. The bombardment had lasted only 12 days when the garrison surrendered. The castle was damaged and became ruinous, and was sold to the Dalrymples in 1699.

Short walk to castle. Explanatory boards and exhibitions. Gift shop. WC. Limited disabled access. Car and coach parking. £.

Open Apr-Sep, daily 9.30-18.30; Oct-Mar, Sat-Wed 9.30-16.30, closed Thu-Fri; last ticket 30 mins before closing; closed 25/26 Dec and 1/2 Jan.

Tel: 01620 892727

Tarbert Castle

[Map: 192; H3] Off A8015, E of Tarbert, Argyll. (NGR: NR 867687 LR: 62)

Above the attractive village of Tarbert, the castle is a ruinous 13th-century royal courtyard stronghold, which was extended by the addition of an outer bailey with towers in the following century. A tower house was built within the walls around 200 years later, but this is also ruinous.

There was a stronghold here of the Dalriadian Scots, which was taken and burnt at least once. Around 1098 Magnus Barelegs, King of Norway, had his longship taken across the isthmus here to symbolise his possession of the Isles. Robert the Bruce strengthened the castle, and James IV extended it again, after capturing it from the MacDonalds, during his campaign to destroy the power of the Lord of the Isles. Walter Campbell of Skipness seized it from its hereditary keeper, the Campbell Earl of Argyll, in 1685 during a rebellion by Argyll. The castle was abandoned by the middle of the 18th century.

Parking in Tarbert.

Access by footpath beside old police station, opposite Fish Quay.

The Binns (NTS)

[Map: 193; H5] Off A904, 3 miles NE of Linlithgow, West Lothian. (NGR: NT 051785 LR: 65)

Set in acres of parkland with excellent views over the Firth of Forth, The Binns is a fine castellated mansion washed in a delicate pink, and was built between 1612 and 1630. There were additions and remodelling later in the 17th century, in the 1740s, and the 1820s. It has fine plaster ceilings from the 17th century; and incorporates part of an old castle.

It was a property of the Livingstones of Kilsyth, but was sold to the Dalziels in 1612. General Tom Dalziel of The Binns was taken prisoner in 1651 at the Battle of Worcester – when in an army under Charles II, which was defeated by Cromwell – but escaped from the Tower of London, and joined the Royalist rising of 1654. He went into exile when the rising collapsed, and served in the Russian army with the Tsar's cossacks, when he is reputed to have roasted prisoners and then later introduced thumb screws to Scotland. Returning after the Restoration, Dalziel was made commander of forces in Scotland from 1666 to 1685. He led the force that defeated the Covenanters at the Battle of Rullion Green in 1666. He also raised the Royal Scots Greys here in 1681.

Collections of portraits, furniture and china. Guided tours. Explanatory displays. WC. Park land. Woodland walk. Disabled access to ground floor and grounds and WC. Car parking. ££.

House open Jun-Sep, Sat-Thu 14.00-17.00, closed Fri; parkland open all year.

Tel: 01506 834255

Thirlestane Castle

[Map: 194; H6] Off A68, E of Lauder, Borders. (NGR: NT 540473 LR: 73)

A magnificent building in a fine setting, Thirlestane Castle incorporates a rectangular tower house or block, dating from the 16th century. It was considerably enlarged in the 1670s by the architect William Bruce. A symmetrical forecourt with wings was also added, and these were extended in the 19th century by David Bryce. A fine 17th-century plaster ceiling survives on the second floor, as do

---

Threave Castle

Baroque plaster ceilings elsewhere.

The present castle was started by Sir John Maitland, James VI's chancellor, although the original castle was two miles away at Old Thirlestane. It was John Maitland, Duke of Lauderdale, a very powerful man in Scotland in the 17th century, who had it remodelled as the building is today. His ghost is said to haunt Thirlestane, as well as St Mary's in Haddington. Bonnie Prince Charlie stayed here in 1745.

Many rooms. Fine 17th-century plasterwork ceilings. Collection of portraits, furniture and china. Exhibition of historical toys and Border country life. Audio-visual presentation. Gift shop. Tea room. WC. Picnic tables. Adventure playground. Woodland walks. Car parking. Coaches by arrangement. Group concessions. £££.

Open Easter, then May-mid Sep, Wed-Fri & Sun 10.30-14.30 (last admission); Jul-Aug, Sun-Fri 10.30-14.30 (last admission).

Tel: 01578 722430   Web: www.thirlestanecastle.co.uk

Threave Castle (HS)

[Map: 195; J4] Off A75, 6 miles W of Dalbeattie, Threave, Dumfries and Galloway.
(NGR: NX 739623   LR: 84)

In a fine location on an island in the River Dee, Threave Castle is a massive ruinous keep, rectangular in plan and dating from the 14th century, which stands within the remains of a courtyard. There was a wall and ditch, with drum towers at each corner, only one of which survives.

An earlier castle here was burnt by Edward Bruce in 1308. The present castle was started by Archibald the Grim (so named because his face was terrible to look upon in battle), 3rd Earl of Douglas and Lord of Galloway. He died at Threave in 1400.

It was from Threave that the young 6th Earl and his brother rode to Edinburgh Castle in 1440 for the Black Dinner, where both were taken out and summarily executed. The 8th Earl was murdered in 1452 by James II at Stirling, after being invited there as an act of reconciliation. The same year Sir Patrick MacLellan of Bombie had been murdered by beheading at Threave. Three years later James II bombarded Threave and the garrison surrendered, but this seems to have been achieved by bribery. The castle went to the Maxwells.

In 1640 the castle was attacked for 13 weeks by an army of Covenanters until forced to surrender. The castle was slighted and partly dismantled. It was given to The National Trust of Scotland in 1948, and is now managed by Historic Scotland.

Sales area. Picnic area. WC. Car and coach parking. £.

Open Apr-Sep, daily 9.30-18.30; last entry 30 mins before closing. Owned by NTS; administered by Historic Scotland – includes walk and short ferry trip.

Tel: 07711 223101 (mobile)

Tolquhon Castle (HS)

[Map: 196; D6] Off A999, 8 miles NE of Inverurie, Tolquhon, Aberdeenshire.
(NGR: NJ 873286 LR: 38)

Tolquhon Castle is a large and attractive courtyard castle in a fine location. It consists of a ruined 15th-century keep in one corner of a courtyard enclosed by later ranges of buildings, which are much better preserved, including a drum-towered gatehouse.

The original keep was built by the Prestons of Craigmillar, but the property passed by marriage to the Forbes family in 1420, and William Forbes, 7th Laird, built the castle as it now is – his carved tomb survives at Tarves. The 6th Laird died at the Battle of Pinkie in 1547. James VI visited in 1589, while the 10th laird saved Charles II's life at the Battle of Worcester in 1651. The Forbes sold the property to the Farquhars in 1716, although the 11th Forbes laird had to be forcibly removed from the castle. The building was used as a farmhouse, but was abandoned and became ruinous.

There are stories of both and a 'White' and a 'Grey Lady' haunting the castle, and there have reputedly been manifestations in recent times.

Sales area. Picnic area. WC. Disabled limited access and WC. Car and coach parking. £.

Open Apr-Sep, daily 9.30-18.30; open Oct-Mar, wknds only 9.30-16.30; last ticket sold 30 mins before closing; closed 25/26 Dec and 1/2 Jan.

Tel: 01651 851286

Torosay Castle

[Map: 197; G3] On A849, 1 mile S of Craignure, Torosay, Mull. (NGR: NM 729353 LR: 49)

Torosay Castle is a fine castellated mansion of 1858, designed by David Bryce for the Campbells of Possel. It was sold to the Guthrie family in 1865, and remains with their descendants. The principal rooms of this stately home are open to the public. The 12-acres of gardens, laid out by Sir Robert

Lorimer in 1899, include formal terraces, an Italian statue walk, Japanese garden, walled garden and woodland, and there are fine views. A working farm has pedigree Highland cattle.

There is a miniature steam railway from Craignure.

Guided tours by arrangement. Gift shop. Tearoom. WC. Disabled access. Pedigree cattle. Isle of Mull Weavers. Miniature steam railway from Craignure. Car and coach parking. Group concessions. ££.

House open April-mid-Oct, daily 10.30-17.30; last entry 30 mins before closing; gardens open all year, daily 9.00-19.00 or daylight hours in winter.

Tel: 01680 812421   Web: www.torosay.com

Traquair House

[Map: 198; H6] Off B709, 1 mile S of Innerleithen, Borders.
(NGR: NT 330354 LR: 73)

Said to be one of the oldest continuously inhabited houses in Scotland, Traquair House is an altered and extended tower house, which may incorporate work from as early as the 12th century. It is now a long and impressive, white-washed edifice, with a steeply pitched roof and crowned by turrets.

Alexander I had a hunting lodge here, but the lands had passed to the Douglases by the 13th century, then through several families until sold to the Stewart Earls of Buchan in 1478.

Mary, Queen of Scots, visited with Lord Darnley in 1566. She left behind a quilt, possibly embroidered by herself and her Four Marys, and the 4th Laird helped her escape from Lochleven Castle after her abdication in 1568. The bed where she slept some of her last nights on Scottish soil was rescued from Terregles and is at Traquair.

Bonnie Prince Charlie stayed in the house in 1745, entering through the Bear Gates. One story is that the 5th Earl closed and locked them after Charlie's departure, swearing they would not be unlocked until a Stewart once more sat on the throne of the country. They are still locked.

The house has a collection of Stewart mementoes, and is owned by the Maxwell Stuarts.

The grounds are said to be haunted by the apparition of Lady Louisa Stewart, sister of the 8th and last Earl of Traquair. It is reported to have been sighted in the grounds around the house, going on her favourite walk by the Quair. She was nearly 100 years old when she died in 1875.

Working 18th-century brewery. Guided tours by arrangement. Explanatory displays. 1745 Cottage

Restaurant. WC. Gardens, woodland walks and maze. Craft workshops. Gift, antique and the Brewery shop. Brewery. Car and coach parking (coaches please book). Group concessions. £££. Accommodation available: contact house.

Open Easter-May & Sep, daily 12.00-17.00, Jun-Aug, daily 10.30-17.00; Nov, wknds only guided tours 12.00-16.00.

Tel: 01896 830323   Web: www.traquair.co.uk

Urquhart Castle (HS)

[Map: 199; D4] Off A82, 1.5 miles E of Drumnadrochit, Urquhart, Highland.
(NGR: NH 531286 LR: 26)

Standing in a picturesque location on the shore of Loch Ness, Urquhart Castle is a 13th-century courtyard castle of enclosure with the remains of a curtain wall and gatehouse. The courtyard encloses ranges of buildings, including a hall and chapel, and has a 16th-century tower house at one end, part of which has collapsed.

The Picts had a fort here in the 6th century, which St Columba may have visited as he is said to have confronted a kelpie or beastie in Loch Ness. The castle was held by the Durwards in the mid 13th century, but passed to the Comyns. It was taken in 1296 by the English, was retaken by the Scots, only to be recaptured by the English in 1303. Five years later it was besieged and seized by the Scots, led by Robert the Bruce.

The castle held out for David II in 1333 against Edward Balliol and Edward III of England. It was captured in 1437 by the Earl of Ross; in 1515 by the MacDonalds; and in 1545 by the MacDonalds and Camerons. In 1644 the castle was sacked by Covenanters, and later passed to the Gordons of Huntly and the Grants. The castle held out against the Jacobites in 1689, but was deliberately slighted a couple of years later when the gatehouse was destroyed by gunpowder.

There have been many reported sightings of the Loch Ness Monster from near the castle.

New visitor centre and car park. Audio-visual show. Walk to castle. Gift shop. Cafe. WC. Car and coach parking. Group concessions. ££.

Open all year: Apr-Sep, daily 9.30-18.30; Oct-Mar, daily 9.30-16.30; last ticket 45 mins before closing; closed 25/26 Dec; open 1/2 Jan: tel for opening times.

Tel: 01456 450551

Winton House

[Map: 200; H6] Off A1, 4.5 miles W of Haddington, Winton, East Lothian. (NGR: NT 439696 LR: 66)

Winton House is a Renaissance mansion, dating from 1620 with later additions, and incorporates a 15th-century castle. There are fine 17th-century plaster ceilings, decorated in honour of Charles I; as well as unique stone twisted chimneys, both added by William Wallace, the king's Master Mason.

The lands were originally held by the Quincy family, but were granted to the Setons after the Quincys were forfeited by Robert the Bruce. Lord Seton built a castle here about 1480, which was

Winton House

later sacked by the English. The Setons were made Earls of Winton in 1600. Charles I visited in 1633.

George, the 5th Earl, was forfeited for his part in the Jacobite Rising of 1715 and imprisoned in the Tower of London after being captured at Preston, although he managed to escape and went to Rome. The property was eventually acquired by the Hamilton Lords Pencaitland about 1779, then passed to the Ogilvys in 1920.

Guided tours. Collections of pictures, furniture, and family exhibitions of costumes and photographs. Tearoom. WC. Picnic area. Terraced gardens and specimen trees. Woodland walks. WC. Limited disabled access, WC. Car and coach parking. Group concessions. ££. Corporate and private hospitality. Accommodation available and weddings, events, etc.

Guided tours only: tel to confirm.

Tel: 01875 340222   Web: www.wintonhouse.co.uk

Borthwick Castle – see next page.

Places to Stay

Many castles and historic houses offer accommodation of one sort or another, and included is only a selection (as space allows) of what is available. This ranges from B&B and self-catering accommodation to luxury hotels and castles which can be rented for exclusive use. Prices vary accordingly. The castle or hotel should be contacted before visiting.

Ackergill Tower
[Map: 201; B5] Off A9, 2.5 miles N of Wick, Ackergill, Caithness. (NGR: ND 352547 LR: 12)
Impressive tower and mansion, long held by the Keiths, and now a conference/hospitality centre offering totally exclusive use.
Tel: 01955 603556   Web: www.ackergill-tower.co.uk

Airth Castle
[Map: 202; H5] Off A905, 4 miles N of Falkirk. (NGR: NS 900869 LR: 65)
Incorporates the 14th-century Wallace's Tower. Held by the Bruces, Elphinstones, Dundases and Graham Earls of Airth, and now a hotel.
Tel: 01324 831411   Web: www.radisson.com

Ardbrecknish House
[Map: 203; G4] Off B840, 7.5 miles N of Inveraray, 2 miles W of Cladich. (NGR: NN 069212 LR: 50)
Incorporates an old castle in the West Tower. Held by the MacArthurs from the 14th century until 1751, and now a hotel.
Tel: 01866 833223   Web: www.loch-awe.co.uk

Barcaldine Castle
[Map: 204; G3] Off A828, 8 miles N of Oban, 4 miles N of Connel, Argyll. (NGR: NM 907405 LR: 49)
Fine restored L-plan tower house, held by the Campbells. Accommodation is available in the castle in July and August.
Tel: 01631 720598   Web: www.barcaldinecastle.co.uk

Barns Tower
[Map: 205; H5] Off A72, 3.5 miles W of Peebles, Barns, Borders. (NGR: NT 215391 LR: 73)
Restored 15th-century tower house, a property of the Burnetts of Burntisland, and built about 1498. Can be rented as holiday accommodation.
Tel: 0845 090 0194   Web: www.vivat.org.uk

Borthwick Castle
[Map: 206; H6] Off A7, 2 miles SE of Gorebridge, Borthwick, Midlothian. (NGR: NT 370597 LR: 66)
Magnificent U-plan tower house, some 110 feet high, built by Sir William Borthwick in 1430. Now used as a hotel.
Tel: 01875 820514   Web: www.celticcastles.co.uk

Busta House
[Map: 207; C6] Off A970, 10 miles NW of Lerwick, Brae, Shetland. (NGR: HU 344670 LR: 3)
Tall harled and white-washed mansion which may date from 1588, a property of the Giffords of Busta, and now a hotel.
Tel: 01806 522506   Web: www.mes.co.uk/busta

Places to Stay

Carnell

[Map: 208; H4] Off A719 or A76, 4 miles SE of Kilmarnock, Ayrshire. (NGR: NS 467323 LR: 70)
Large mansion with a 15th-century keep at its core. Long held by the Wallaces. The house is available to rent as holiday accommodation.
Tel: 01563 884236   Web: www.carnellestates.com

Carriden House

[Map: 209; H5] Off A904, 1.5 miles E of Bo'ness, Carriden, Falkirk. (NGR: NT 026808 LR: 65)
Turreted tower house and large mansion, held by the Viponts, Cockburns, Hamiltons and others. Accommodation is available and suitable for weddings.
Tel: 01506 829811

Castle Levan

[Map: 210; H4] Off A770, 1.5 miles SW of Gourock, Renfrewshire. (NGR: NS 216764 LR: 63)
Strong L-plan tower house of the Mortons, then the Semples and Stewarts of Inverkip. B&B accommodation is available.
Tel: 01475 659154   Web: www.castle-levan.com

Castle Stuart

[Map: 211; D5] Off B9039, 6 miles NE of Inverness, Highlands. (NGR: NH 742498 LR: 27)
Large and impressive tower house. Lands were held by the Mackintoshes, but given to the Stewarts. Overnight accommodation available by reservation.
Tel: 01463 790745   Web: www.castlestuart.com (also www.brigadoon.co.uk)

Castle of Park

[Map: 212; J4] Off A75, 0.5 miles W of Glenluce village, Galloway. (NGR: NX 189571 LR: 82)
Restored L-plan tower, built by Hay of Park, but passed to the Cunninghams. Can be rented through the Landmark Trust.
Tel: 01628 825925   Web: www.landmarktrust.org.uk

Castle of Park

[Map: 213; D6] Off A9023, 4 miles NW of Aberchirder, Banff and Buchan. (NGR: NJ 587571 LR: 29)
Z-plan tower house in 1563, extended in later centuries, held by the Gordons. Open all year to residents by arrangement: painting and writing courses.
Tel: 01466 751667   Web: www.castleofpark.net

Comlongon Castle

[Map: 214; I5] Off B724, 8 miles SE of Dumfries, Dumfries and Galloway. (NGR: NY 079690 LR: 85)
Massive tower house and large later mansion stands nearby. Held by the Murrays of Cockpool, haunted by a 'Green Lady' and the mansion is now a hotel.
Tel: 01387 870283   Web: www.comlongon.co.uk

Craighall-Rattray

[Map: 215; G5] Off A93, 2 miles N of Blairgowrie, Perthshire. (NGR: NO 175480 LR: 53)
Baronial mansion incorporating part of a tower house, long a property of the Rattray family. Accommodation is available.
Tel: 01250 874749   Web: www.craighall.co.uk

Culcreuch Castle

[Map: 216; H4] Off B822, 11 miles E of Stirling, 0.5 miles N of Fintry. (NGR: NS 620876 LR: 57)
Fine altered and extended castle of the Galbraiths, then Napiers and Speirs family. Now a hotel, and stands in a country park open to the public.
Tel: 01360 860228/555   Web: www.culcreuch.com

Culloden House

[Map: 217; D5] Off A96, 3.5 miles E of Inverness, Culloden, Highland. (NGR: NH 721465 LR: 27)
Old mansion with cellars from a tower house. Held by the Forbeses, but now used as a hotel.
Tel: 01463 790461   Web: www.cullodenhouse.co.uk

Dalcross Castle

[Map: 218; D5] Off B9006, 7 miles E of Inverness, 1.5 miles SW of Croy. (NGR: NH 779483 LR: 27)
Restored L-plan tower house, held by the Frasers of Lovat, who built the castle, then the Mackintoshes. Self-catering accommodation is available.
Tel: 01738 451600   Web: www.scotland-holiday-homes.co.uk/inverness-shire/dalcross.html

Dalhousie Castle

[Map: 219; H6] Off B704, 3 miles S of Dalkeith, Bonnyrigg, Midlothian. (NGR: NT 320636 LR: 66)
Fine building incorporating an ancient castle into the large baronial mansion. Built by the Ramsays, later Earls of Dalhousie, and now used as a hotel.
Tel: 01875 820153   Web: www.dalhousiecastle.co.uk

Dornoch Castle or Palace

[Map: 220; C5] Off A949, Dornoch, near cathedral, Sutherland. (NGR: NH 797897 LR: 21)
Strong tower of five storeys along with round stair-tower. Built by the Bishops of Caithness, but passed to Earls of Sutherland. Now used as a hotel.
Tel: 01862 810216   Web: www.dornochcastlehotel.com

Drumkilbo

[Map: 221; G5] Off A92, 6 miles NE of Coupar Angus, Perthshire. (NGR: NO 304449 LR: 53)
Mansion incorporating some of an ancient tower house. Held by the Tyries and the Nairne family.
The house is available to rent on an exclusive basis.
Tel: 01828 640445   Web: www.drumkilbo.com

Duns Castle

[Map: 222; H6] Off A6112, 1 mile NW of Duns, Borders. (NGR: NT 777544 LR: 67)
Altered and extended castle, dating from the 14th century, and standing in Duns Castle Country Park. Held by the Hays. Accommodation available.
Tel: 01361 883211   Web: www.dunscastle.co.uk

Erchless Castle

[Map: 223; D4] Off A831, 8 miles SW of Beauly, Erchless, Highland. (NGR: NH 410408 LR: 26)
Extended L-plan tower house from the 16th century. Held by the Frasers, then the Chisholms until 1935. Accommodation available in North Wing.
Tel: 01738 451600   Web: www.scotland-holiday-homes.co.uk/inverness-shire/erchless.html

Ethie Castle

[Map: 224; G6] Off A92, 5 miles NE of Arbroath, Angus. (NGR: NO 688468 LR: 54)
Large castle and mansion, dating from the 15th century, and held by the Beatons, then the Carnegies until the 20th century. Accommodation available.
Tel: 01241 830434   Web: www.ethiecastle.com

Fenton Tower

[Map: 225; H6] Off B1347, 2 miles S of North Berwick, East Lothian. (NGR: NT 543822 LR: 66)
Restored L-plan tower house. Held by the Fentons, Whitelaws, Carmichaels, Erskines and Maxwells.
Features in Balamory. Luxury accommodation available.
Tel: 01620 890089   Web: www.fentontower.co.uk

Places to Stay

Fernie Castle

[Map: 226; G6] On A914, 4 miles W of Cupar, Fernie, Fife. (NGR: NO 316147 LR: 59)
Fine altered L-plan tower house, dating from 16th century, and held by the Balfours and other families. Has stories of a 'Green Lady'. Now a hotel.
Tel: 01337 810381   Web: www.ferniecastle.demon.co.uk

Fordyce Castle

[Map: 227; D6] Off A98, 2.5 miles SW of Portsoy, Fordyce, Aberdeenshire. (NGR: NJ 556638 LR: 29)
Turreted and extended L-plan tower, from 16th-century. Held by Dunbars, Ogilvies and Menzies family. Part can be rented as holiday accommodation.
Tel: 01261 843722   Web: www.fordycecastle.co.uk

Guthrie Castle

[Map: 228; F6] Off A932, 6.5 miles E of Forfar, Guthrie, Angus. (NGR: NO 563505 LR: 54)
Impressive castle and mansion, which dates from the 15th century, and was a property of the Guthries until the 20th century. Accommodation available.
Tel: 01241 828691   Web: www.guthriecastle.com

Hallbar Tower

[Map: 229; H5] Off B7056, 2 miles SW of Carluke, Lanarkshire. (NGR: NS 839471 LR: 72)
Restored tower house, dating from the 16th century. Held by the Douglases, Stewarts, Maitlands and Lockharts. Holiday accommodation is available.
Tel: 0845 090 0194   Web: www.vivat.org.uk

Houston House

[Map: 230; H5] Off A899, Uphall, West Lothian. (NGR: NT 058716 LR: 65)
Large castle and mansion, ranged around a courtyard. Held by the Houstons and then later the Sharps until 1945. Now a hotel.
Tel: 01506 853831   Web: www.macdonald-hotels.co.uk

Kilravock Castle

[Map: 231; D5] Off B9091, 6 miles SW of Nairn, Kilravock, Highland. (NGR: NH 814493 LR: 27)
Magnificent castle, dating from the 15th century, and long a property of the Roses. Guest house, sports centre and youth hostel.
Tel: 01667 493258   Web: www.kilravockcastle.com

Kinnaird Castle

[Map: 232; F6] Off A934, 5.5 miles W of Montrose, Angus. (NGR: NO 634571 LR: 54)
Impressive mansion of the 19th century, built on site of an old castle. Long a property of the Carnegies, Earls of Southesk. Accommodation available.
Tel: 01828 633383   Web: www.scottscastles.com

Law Castle

[Map: 233; H4] Off B7047, 0.5 miles NE of West Kilbride, Ayrshire. (NGR: NS 211484 LR: 63)
Stout rectangular keep, dating from the 15th century, and held by the Boyds and then the Bontines. Accommodation available.
Tel: 01505 703 119   Web: www.lawcastle.com

Leny House

[Map: 234; G4] Off A84, 1.5 miles W of Callander, Leny, Stirlingshire. (NGR: NN 613089 LR: 57)
Old castle and turreted mansion. Lands held by the Leny family, but were long a property of the Buchanans. Now a hotel.
Tel: 01877 331078   Web: www.lenyestate.com

Liberton Tower

[Map: 235; H5] Off A701, Liberton, SE of Edinburgh. (NGR: NT 265697 LR: 66)
Small, plain but impressive keep from the 15th century, recently restored. Held by the Dalmahoys and then the Littles. Available for let.
Tel: 0990 851133   Web: www.cospt.fsnet.co.uk

Maryculter House

[Map: 236; E6] Off B9077, South Deeside Road, 8 miles SW of Aberdeen. (NGR: NO 845999 LR: 38)
Fine altered and extended mansion. Built on site of house of the Knights Templars and then the Menzies family. Now a hotel.
Tel: 01224 732124   Web: www.maryculterhousehotel.co.uk

Meldrum House

[Map: 237; D6] Off A947, 1 mile N of Oldmeldrum, Aberdeenshire. (NGR: NJ 812291 LR: 38)
Large mansion with work from an ancient castle. Held by the Meldrums, Setons and Urquharts, and has stories of a ghost. Now a hotel.
Tel: 01651 872294   Web: www.meldrumhouse.co.uk

Melville Castle

[Map: 238; H6] Off A7, 1.5 miles W of Dalkeith, Melville, Midlothian. (NGR: NT 310669 LR: 66)
Large castellated mansion on site of old stronghold. Held by the Rosses, Rennies and then the Dundases. Recently restored and now a hotel.
Tel: 0131 654 0088   Web: www.melvillecastle.com

Menie House

[Map: 239; E7] Off A92, 2 miles north of Balmedie, Aberdeenshire. (NGR: NJ 978206 LR: 38)
Fine mansion with old work and stands on the site of a castle. Held by the Forbeses, and said to have a 'Green Lady'. Accommodation available.
Tel: 01358 742885   Web: www.meniehouse.com

Minard Castle

[Map: 240; G3] Off A83, 8 miles NE of Lochgilphead, Argyll. (NGR: NR 973943 LR: 55)
Mansion, dating from the 18th century but later altered and extended. Held by Campbells and Lloyds. B&B (Apr-Oct); self-catering accommodation available.
Tel: 01546 886272   Web: www.minardcastle.com

Old Mansion House, Auchterhouse

[Map: 241; G6] Off B954, 7 miles NE of Dundee, Auchterhouse, Angus. (NGR: NO 332373 LR: 53)
Mansion incorporating work from an old castle. Held by the Ramsays, then the Stewarts, Maules and Ogilvies. Now a hotel.
Tel: 01382 320366   Web: visitscotland.com/oldmansionhouse

Ord House

[Map: 242; D4] Off A832, 1 mile W of Muir of Ord, Ord House, Highland. (NGR: NH 514505 LR: 26)
Mansion dating from 1810 or earlier but later altered and extended. Held by the Mackenzies, said to be haunted by the ghost of a lady, and now a hotel.
Tel: 01463 870492   Web: www.ord-house.com

Pittodrie House

[Map: 243; D6] Off A96, 5 miles NW of Inverurie, Aberdeenshire (NGR: NJ 697241 LR: 38)
Altered mansion incorporating an L-plan tower house. Held by the Erskines, said to be haunted, and now a hotel.
Tel: 01467 681444   Web: www.macdonald-hotels.co.uk

Places to Stay

Plean Castle
[Map: 244; H5] Off B9124, 6 miles SE of Stirling, Plean. (NGR: NS 850870 LR: 65)
Altered castle from the 15th century, recently restored. Held by the Airths, Somervilles, Nicholsons and Elphinstones. Accommodation available.
Tel: 01786 480480   Web: www.aboutscotland.co.uk/stirling/plane.html

Rosslyn Castle
[Map: 245; H6] Off B7006, 2 miles S of Loanhead, Roslin, Midlothian. (NGR: NT 274628 LR: 66)
Remains of a once mighty castle, mostly ruinous but a block of which is still in excellent condition. Long a property of the Sinclairs. Accommodation available.
Tel: 01628 825925   Web: www.landmarktrust.org.uk

Rumgally House
[Map: 246; G6] Off B940, 2 miles E of Cupar, Rumgally House, Fife. (NGR: NO 407149 LR: 59)
Altered house incorporating L-plan tower house. Held by the Scotts, Wemyss family and the MacGills. B&B accommodation available.
Tel: 01334 653388   Web: www.sol.co.uk/r/rumgally/

Saddell Castle
[Map: 247; H3] Off B842, 8 miles N of Campbeltown, Kintyre. (NGR: NR 789316 LR: 68)
Substantial keep, dating from the 15th century and built by the Bishops of Argyll. Later held by the Campbells and Ralstons. Can be rented.
Tel: 01628 825925   Web: www.landmarktrust.org.uk

Shieldhill
[Map: 248; H5] Off B7016, 3 miles NW of Biggar, Quothquan, Lanarkshire. (NGR: NT 008407 LR: 72)
Mansion incorporating a strong castle, from as early as the 12th century. Held by the Chancellors and said to be haunted by a 'Grey Lady'. Now a hotel.
Tel: 01899 220035   Web: www.shieldhill.co.uk

Skelmorlie Castle
[Map: 249; H4] Off A78, 4.5 miles N of Largs, Ayrshire. (NGR: NS 195658 LR: 63)
Turreted tower house, dating from the 16th century, and owned by the Cunninghams and the Mont-gomerys. Self-catering accommodation available.
Tel: 01475 521616   Web: www.aboutscotland.com/ayrshire/skelmorlie.html

Tulloch Castle
[Map: 250; D4] Off A862, 1 mile N of Dingwall, Ross, Highland. (NGR: NH 547605 LR: 21)
Castle and mansion dating from the 16th century or earlier, and held by the Inneses, Bains and Davidsons. Said to have a 'Green Lady'. Now a hotel.
Tel: 01349 861325   Web: www.tulloch.co.uk

Some of the sites listed in the main text also offer accommodation.

Glossary

Angle-Turret Turret crowning corner of a building

Arcade A series of arches supported by columns

Arch A self-supporting structure capable of carrying a load over an opening

Attic The top storey entirely within a gabled roof; also garret

Bailey A defensible area enclosed by a wall or palisade and a ditch

Barmkin *(Scots)* Courtyard

Bartizan Turret crowning corner of a building

Basement The lowest storey of a building, sometimes below ground

Battlement A crenellated parapet, allowing defenders to shoot between the solid sections

Caphouse A small watch-chamber at the top of a turnpike stair, often opening into the parapet walk

Castle A stronghold or residence of a nobleman or landowner

Castellations Battlements and turrets

Corbiestepped *(Scots)* Squared stones forming steps upon a gable

Corbel A projecting bracket supporting other stonework or timbers

Courtyard castle Usually a castle of some size and importance built around a central courtyard, often with a tower or keep, gatehouse, and ranges of buildings

Crenellations Battlements

Crowstepped Squared stones forming steps upon a gable (corbiestepped)

Curtain Wall A high enclosing stone wall

Doocot *(Scots)*/**Dovecote** Building for housing doves, which were used for eggs and meat

E-plan tower house Tower house with a main block and at least two wings at right angles, dating from the 16th and 17th centuries

Enceinte The line of the wall encircling a fortress

Gable A vertical wall or other vertical surface, frequently triangular, at the end of a pitched roof. In Scotland often corbiestepped

Gallery A balcony or passage, often with seats, sometimes overlooking a great hall or garden

Garret The top storey of a building within the roof

Keep Strong stone tower. A citadel or ultimate strong point, normally with a vaulted basement, hall and additional storeys. also donjon

L-plan tower house   Distinctive Scottish form of the tower house in which a wing was added at right angles to the main tower block

Main Block   Principal part of a castle, usually containing the hall and lord's chamber

Moat   A ditch, water filled or dry, around an enclosure

Motte   A steeply sided flat-topped mound

Motte and bailey   A defence system, Roman in origin, consisting of an earth motte (mound) carrying a wooden tower with a bailey (open court) with an enclosing ditch and palisade

Palace   An old Scottish term for a hall or residential block; also Place

Parapet   A wall for protection at any sudden drop, but defensive in a castle

Pit-Prison   A dark prison only reached by a hatch in a vault

Place   An old Scottish term for a hall or residential block; also Palace

Portcullis   A wooden and/or iron gate designed to rise and fall in vertical grooves

Postern   A secondary gateway or doorway; a back entrance

Rampart   A stone or earth wall surrounding a stronghold

Royal castle   A castle held by a keeper or constable for the monarch

Scale-and-platt   Stair with short straight flights and turnings at landings

Slight   To destroy a castle's defences

Tempera   Form of wall painting directly onto wet plaster

Tower House   House with the main rooms stacked vertically usually with a hall over a vaulted basement with further storeys above

T-plan   House or tower where the main (long) block has a wing or tower (usually for the stair) in the centre of one front

Turnpike stair   Spiral stair around a newel or central post

Turret   A small tower usually attached to a building

Vault   An arched ceiling of stone

Yett   A strong hinged gate made of interwoven iron bars

Walled Enclosure   A simple castle, normally where a wall encloses a rock or island with a wooden hall and buildings

Z-plan   Distinctive Scottish form of the tower house where two corner towers were added to the main tower block at diagonally opposite corners

Index by Family & Clan Name

Index

Index

Bold entry refers to sites in the main part of the book (not the places to stay)
Bold page no. refers to the first page of the entry; underlined no. to a photo of the site

Index